MAPPING THE AIRWAYS

Paul Jarvis

AMBERLEY

In association with **BRITISH AIRWAYS**

First published 2016

Amberley Publishing
The Hill, Stroud
Gloucestershire, GL5 4EP

www.amberley-books.com

Copyright © Paul Jarvis & British Airways, 2016

The right of Paul Jarvis & British Airways to be identified as the Author of this work
has been asserted in accordance with the Copyrights, Designs and Patents Act 1988

ISBN 978 1 4456 5464 5 (paperback)
ISBN 978 1 4456 5465 2 (ebook)

British Library Cataloguing in Publication Data.
A catalogue record for this book is available from the British Library.

Typesetting by Amberley Publishing.
Printed in the UK.

CONTENTS

FOREWORD

British Airways has the richest history in world aviation. I say that not out of chauvinism but out of honest reflection on the contribution to global transport made by my airline as we know it today and its forerunner companies.

Barely a decade and a half after the dawn of commercial flying in Europe, Britain's Imperial Airways had an unparalleled route network that stretched to southern and eastern Africa, the Middle East, India, Hong Kong and Australia. Journeys that would previously have taken several weeks could be accomplished in a few days.

Post-war, the story of expansion and innovation continued. Imperial had evolved into three new nationalised companies, BEA (for flights within Europe), BSAA (for South America and the Caribbean) and BOAC (for the rest of the world). Regular services across the Atlantic, to the Far East and all points in between became the norm. In 1952, BOAC started the world's first scheduled jet service, flying an aircraft that cruised at 500 mph – comparable with today's airliners and far faster than its predecessors. Flying times tumbled and the world started to shrink.

In 1958, BOAC beat the combined might of the American carriers to operate the first jet service between London and New York. When the jumbo jet started the era of mass long-haul travel, BOAC was quick to grasp its potential and large orders followed.

Forty years ago this year, BOAC and BEA were formally brought together as British Airways. With nearly 200 destinations in 88 countries, it had the most extensive route network in the world. Another aviation first soon ensued with the launch of supersonic travel. Though Concorde retired a decade ago, its iconic image lives on around the globe as a lasting symbol of British Airways' innovation.

That pioneering tradition has gone on, finding different forms of expression as times change. Privatisation, fully flat beds, online check-in, environmental performance – British Airways is proud of its record as an industry leader right up to the present day.

That is part of the culture that underpins our motto, 'To Fly. To Serve'. Those words were painted on our early aircraft and are emblazoned on our fuselages today. Whoever we are, our history is always part of us. The history of British Airways is indeed rich, and there is no better demonstration of that fact than this fascinating book.

Keith Williams
Executive Chairman, British Airways, March 2016

ACKNOWLEDGEMENTS

The idea for this book came from a realisation that there were quite a number of books out there relating to mapping all sorts of things from railways to roads and even British history, but none that I had seen on what I call Mapping the Airways. I mean that in the widest literal sense; in essence, the use of maps in UK civil aviation primarily as a promotional medium but also as a practical device for finding the way.

Fortuitously, as curator of the British Airways Heritage Collection, I've access to a wide range of media that show maps in different forms – from advertising posters to all manner of informational and promotional literature right down to real maps used to plot an aircraft's route and landing place. I'm also very keen on maps and as a sort of geographer like nothing more than poring over a map, the more detailed the better. Writing this book was therefore more of a delight than a challenge, although when trying to interpret why a map had been used in a particular way it was soon clear I did not know quite as much as I had thought.

What shone through, however, was the innovative and creative ways that maps have been used in promoting the business of commercial aviation. In the air, pilots have progressed from the use of bookshop road maps in the 1920s to twenty-first-century GPS navigation. Many of the artworks and charts are unique in themselves and we are very fortunate they have survived at all. As part of our collection they represent a major national asset, given that for nearly seventy years between 1924 and 1987 British Airways and its predecessor airlines were the nationalised air carriers of the United Kingdom.

Putting all this material together was, as ever, a team effort. The collection's team of volunteers have all had a part to play in this story, using their particular skills and knowledge. Christine Quick's patience in scanning and preparing several hundreds of images while I worried over which ones to use has to be commended. Adrian Constable's photography and Bob Petrie's digital imaging skills also allowed many images to be seen probably for the first time for over ninety years. Jim Davies's and Alan Cavender's diligent fact-checking and proofreading also kept the text accurate and on track.

Paul Jarvis
British Airways Heritage Collection

BRUSSELS–CONGO IN 4½ DAYS

Our story begins in the early years of the twentieth century with an airline advertising poster from around late 1919 or early 1920. We can't be precise. This poster, from British Airways' predecessor airline Aircraft Transport & Travel, is a good starting point because, prior to the start of AT&T's commercial passenger operations on 25 August 1919, there really were no airways by any airline of any consequence to map. Aviation was still in its infancy, although technically and militarily it had grown significantly during the years of the First World War, between 1914 and 1918. Before that, aviation of any sort was often still experimental, with aircraft hardly able to fly with one person – the pilot – let alone any passengers.

AT&T's poster, while not containing a map of any description, highlights its very first route between London and Paris. It hardly needed a map to show prospective customers where they were going and, I suspect, the commercial artist who painted the poster probably thought similarly. The most obvious thing to illustrate was the service product itself, an aeroplane – in this case a De Havilland DH16 four-seater – and the eye-catching, iconic landmarks of St Paul's Cathedral and the Eiffel Tower; together, they could leave no one in doubt what the service was about and where it was going. These sort of almost storybook-style illustrations, coupled with an appropriate message, became key points for airline advertising for many decades.

Fifteen years later and we come to the title of this chapter. Imperial Airways, another predecessor airline of British Airways, is flying across continents. How best,

Where it all began on 25 August 1919: AT&T's stylised poster from late 1919/early 1920 set a pattern of commercial aviation advertising and promotion that lasted into the early 1970s. (MB)

then, to advertise in the 1930s an air journey from the heart of Europe to the heart of Africa? This was a quite long and complex journey in those days, involving several changes of aircraft and even two days on the train between Paris and Brindisi in Italy. Apart from illustrating any text, a map would seem a natural inclusion to put elements of the journey into a neat visual context. A map was not used, however, but a timetable, a very useful figurative guide used successfully for many years by other transport modes, especially the railways. It was a very obvious thing to copy. In fact, from a purely practical perspective, a timetable was better than a map because it could show very accurately the various combinations on this complex journey of route, days of travel and flight timings. Personally, I'd still have preferred a map (or at least a map as well), but the inclusion of a timetable allowed more specific information to be added which, for a complex journey, made a lot of sense.

As commercial airline route networks rapidly grew during the 1920s and 1930s, maps, both geographic and diagrammatic, would begin to be used widely in all sorts of airline promotional material. Not only posters, but passenger information leaflets, timetables and other ephemera often contained a map; but why do this? It was not that airline customers did not know where they were going, but air travel, even on a fairly simple route, brings an inevitable complexity that a map can put into a contextual and relatively simple visual format that speaks volumes about the journey to be undertaken. Coupled with illustrative art, a map can become a visual joy that both promotes and informs, creating a lasting

This poster advertisement from 1935 by Imperial Airways' advertising company, Stuarts Agency, incorporates a route timetable in place of a map, probably due to the complexity of the journey's possible route combinations. It also includes the same sort of stylised combination of images as those used in the AT&T poster fifteen years earlier, i.e. images of the points of origin and destination and one of the principal aircraft of Imperial Airways' fleet, a Handley Page HP42. Although a biplane and rapidly becoming obsolete by the standards of the day, with a top speed of only around 100 mph, the illustrator has drawn the image in a way to suggest speed and highlighting that the journey would (only) take four and a half days. This was an unthinkable length of time by today's standards but a huge improvement in travelling time in the 1930s for a journey that otherwise would take around two weeks by ship. Interestingly, Stuarts Agency have been rather creative by emphasising the four and a half days. It suggests that was the time it took to reach the Congo but without stating exactly where in that country (at the time part of Belgian overseas territory). Imperial Airways never flew directly to the Congo, and even the first two sectors from Brussels to Paris and then on to Brindisi were by train, with two overnight stops en route. The nearest point to the Congo border would have been at Entebbe (then in Nyasaland, now Malawi) and that was reached after another three night stops; a connecting flight, or more likely an overland journey, would then have been necessary to reach any major town in the Congo, so the journey looks more like five days at least. (Severin)

impact; is it any wonder that, wherever they were used, they were often taken by passengers to commemorate their journeys?

For Imperial Airways' advertising agencies of the time, their options would have seemed to be limited only by the imaginations of their creatives and their artistic skills. All the tools they needed were in place: illustrations, maps both geographical and diagrammatic, and a timetable, where required. From a sales perspective, such advertising stimulated the imagination at a time when air travel was not the mass-market phenomenon it became in the later decades of the twentieth century and the world was a less well-known place to the general public; the far-flung outposts of the British Empire were known, if at all, largely from history and geography books, although there was a wide interest in matters abroad and maps were a well-known illustrative medium to many people. Illustrative advertising in the 1920s and 1930s provided an opportunity to both promote an air service generally and to highlight exactly where a particular country or destination was, along with any points of interest to be experienced en route, on a journey that could, for example, take ten and a half days – as it did to reach Australia.

The progressive use of maps for promotion and information seems very similar to me to the development of seventeenth-century strip maps, distinctive way markers and points of interest being added along a route, the difference being that these were not to guide an aircraft's pilots but to inform their passengers. Many airlines offered their passengers map guides, often beautifully illustrated. Imperial Airways even produced multi-page folded strip maps for many of their long routes, with cartoon illustrations or photographs about aviation points of interest on the reverse.

The sort of interesting places and people that air travellers experienced in the early days of air travel are rarely touched upon in a twenty-first-century air journey; flights are often many hours in duration and, in airline parlance, 'point-to- point', i.e. not stopping between the point of departure and point of destination, such as London to Tokyo. In the early 1950s, before the introduction of commercial jet airliners, it could take eighty-six hours to reach Japan with up to eight stops for refuelling en route.

Of course, in aviation traditional and un-stylised maps also have a very practical application, just as in the maritime world. When aviation developed in the early twentieth century the maritime world provided a useful guide to early aviators both in finding the way and in the practicalities of operating what were sometimes called, especially in the case of flying boats, 'ships of the air'. Maritime terminology was also widely adopted - aircraft have captains and crew who serve food from galleys to passengers in cabins sitting either on the port or starboard side of an aircraft. In the larger flying boats of the 1930s there were even promenade decks on which passengers could socialise and, literally, watch through portholes as the world slid slowly by a few thousand feet below. In the early days of aviation, before more sophisticated technology was developed, aircraft navigators even used the same navigation charts as ships; when flying boats were first developed in the early 1920s, the relationship grew ever stronger, not least in using charts to find safe anchorages and passageways at the ports of arrival and destination. Nowadays, a computer logs a flightpath's way markers and airline navigators are a long-departed breed of aviators.

The first part of this book is a nostalgic look back at the emotional appeal and originality of the artworks used to advertise and promote airline services from the 1920s to the 1970s, in particular by the use of maps both in a traditional and stylised format. Where used in a strict geographical sense they are not art but used purely to illustrate the depth and spread of an airline's route network, a simplicity and precision beloved of an airline's planners putting its services clearly and simply into a worldwide or regional context. Simplicity and precision, however, is not always the best way to sell air services. As previously mentioned, it needs the wealth of creativity of an advertising agency and their artists to inform and stimulate prospective customers; in the earlier part of the twentieth century, a map provided a useful tool to achieve that. It was, if you like, an integral part of the advertiser's storytelling.

The second part of this book looks at the use of traditional maps and charts by commercial airlines. Up to the 1960s aircraft crews invariably needed a navigator, whose main role was to use maps and charts to guide the aircraft's crew along designated flightpaths accurately and safely. While long since replaced, firstly by pilots carrying out the role and, in more recent years, by computers, it is nevertheless interesting to note that only fairly recently have back-up, hard-copy maps and charts been replaced entirely by the introduction of GPS navigation.

The main body of this book is a collection of illustrated or stylised maps taken from the British Airways Heritage Collection archives and mainly comprising material from British Airways' predecessor companies Imperial Airways (1924–40), British Overseas Airways Corporation (BOAC, 1940–74), British European Airways (BEA, 1946–74) and British South American Airways (BSAA, 1946–49). Together they represent a collection of interest and importance in the use of maps in the context of civil aviation by the UK's principal national airline and its predecessors.

By 1926, Imperial Airways had started to use maps in its general posters but without much imagination. Imperial Airways had only been formed in 1924 and in its early years was more concerned with establishing its air services to the few European points it then served than any form of innovative advertising. Apart from a few dotted lines linking London with Paris and a rather childlike drawing of an aircraft, there is little else to encourage travel apart from one very important point the advertisement does make – the journey time was only two and a half hours by air but seven and a quarter hours by train and ship, a considerable saving and a unique selling point that Imperial Airways heavily promoted. These maps were not giveaways but neatly folded into a small advertising brochure and sold for 6d (£1.36 in 2015).

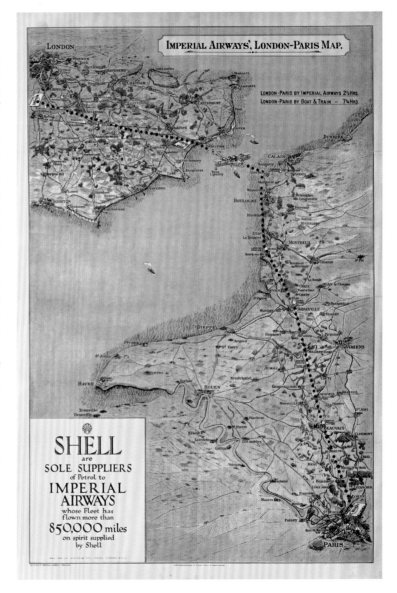

Le Confort

SUR LES AILES DES

Imperial Airways

AFRIQUE · INDES · EXTREME-ORIENT · AUSTRALIE

de mettre quelques jours au lieu de quelques semaines

MAP OF THE AIR ROUTE

1934-35 CAIRO-CAPETOWN

IMPERIAL AIRWAYS

PRICE 2/-

LEE·ELLIOTT

This spread, overleaf: Imperial Airways' strip map of its Cairo to Cape Town route, neatly packaged in a soft cover, rather like an Ordnance Survey map, was sold to passengers for 2s (£6.38 in 2015, so quite expensive). The map legend goes into some detail on how to use the map and contains photographs and a text on points of interest to be seen en route. The pilot would often make sure that he overflew these points to maximise his passengers' viewing opportunities; on Imperial's large Short 'C' Class flying boats the views seen from their promenade deck cabins would have been magnificent. The reverse of the map strips were often separately illustrated or used for advertising; in this case, cartoon-like drawings by Edward Bawden were used illustrating text about aviation 'firsts' such as Bleriot's crossing of the English Channel. Bawden was used by Stuarts Agency for Imperial's advertising and he also illustrated their 'crossing the line' certificate for those passengers crossing the Equator on the Entebbe–Kisumu sector of their journey. (Left: Theyre Lee-Elliot; overleaf: Edward Bawden)

ABOUT THE MAP AND HOW TO READ IT

The map in this folder is as far as possible a reproduction of the large scale flying maps produced by RAYNOIL Maps Ltd. for Imperial Airways pilots, but on the small scale of 75 miles to one inch. Magnetic flying courses are given, and lines of magnetic variation are shewn throughout the map, and vary from 0° at Cairo to 24° at Cape Town.

To follow the course from, say, Cairo to Assiut, hold the folder with the map running away from you, and the red line of flight pointing in the direction the aeroplane is going ; you then have a miniature of the country over which you are travelling.

Ascertain from one of the officers the approximate ground speed of the liner ; then a simple calculation will shew you when you may expect to see coming into view and immediately ahead Assiut, and the Barrage over the Nile. In this way you will be able to check your position along the whole route, and complete your daily diary in the space provided for this purpose.

CAIRO-CAPE TOWN AIR ROUTE
(Heliopolis - Wingfield.)
5468 MILES

REFERENCE

Air Route ....
Aerodromes & Heights .... CAIRO ⊚(50')
Landing Grounds .... Luxor ●
Bearings & Distances (Outward) .... 185° 205Mls.
             ,,   (Homeward) ...... 5° 205Mls.
Prohibited Areas ....
Roads ....
Railways ....
Rivers, Lakes, Canals ....
Frontiers .... +++++++
Note: *All bearings are magnetic.*

SCALE
MILES 0   50   100   200 MILES
       0 50 100   200   300 KILOMETRES

PRINTED IN GREAT BRITAIN &
PUBLISHED BY "RAYNOIL" MAPS LTD.
6, TAVISTOCK SQUARE LONDON W.C.1.

AIR VIEWS BY AEROFILMS LTD. LONDON WC.2

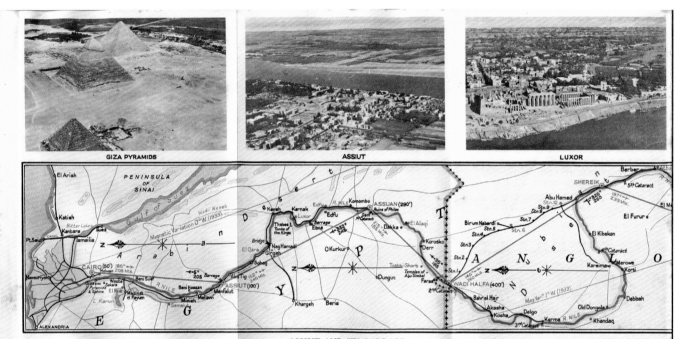

GIZA PYRAMIDS   ASSIUT   LUXOR

CAIRO AND THE PYRAMIDS

From Cairo you fly due south and follow closely the Valley of the Nile. You may see beneath you to the west the Giza Pyramids, the largest of which (Cheops) is nearly 500 feet in height : then further south the ancient step pyramid of Sakara, built some 5,000 years ago by King Zoser. Further on again, to the west, lies Lake Karun, and next to it the fertile oases of Fayum

ASSIUT AND ITS BARRAGE

Your next stop, Assiut, is famous for its Barrage across the Nile, which here turns away from our course in a vast loop.

Far to the left you pass Luxor, and almost beneath you lies Thebes, with its Tombs of the Kings (the site of the Tutankhamen excavations) and the twin Memnon Colossi of Amenhotep III and his Consort

TEMPLES OF LUXOR AND KARNAK

These famous remains, as well as the Temples of Luxor and Karnak and Sethos, are actually best approached from your next stop (Assouan). Before reaching Assouan, however, you will fly across a rugged gorge, faced by black basalt hills, and a little later you will see the Nile again and the Railway which follows it along its Eastern side from Luxor

A
CERTIFICATE OF
CONTEMPORARY TRAVEL

This is to certify that

_____

has flown over the equator in the *Empire* flying-
boat the _____
thus becoming one of the progressive band of
travellers who cross the line by air. Over the waters
of Lake Victoria, the Lingga Archipelago, the *Empire*
flying-boats pass in a moment from hemisphere to
hemisphere, beyond the zone whose dwellers recognize
no alteration in the length of night and day

'Born with the sun they travelled a short way towards the sun,
And left the vivid air signed with their honour'
Stephen Spender

Longitude _____
Latitude zero
_____ 193____

_____ Commander

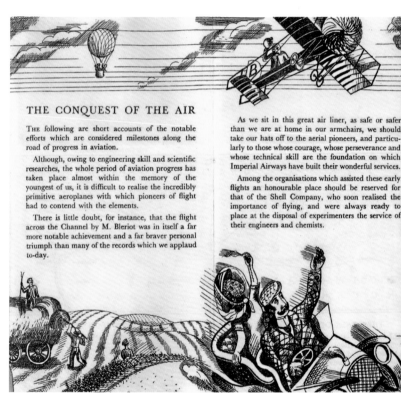

THE CONQUEST OF THE AIR

THE following are short accounts of the notable
efforts which are considered milestones along the
road of progress in aviation.

Although, owing to engineering skill and scientific
researches, the whole period of aviation progress has
taken place almost within the memory of the
youngest of us, it is difficult to realise the incredibly
primitive aeroplanes with which pioneers of flight
had to contend with the elements.

There is little doubt, for instance, that the flight
across the Channel by M. Bleriot was in itself a far
more notable achievement and a far braver personal
triumph than many of the records which we applaud
to-day.

As we sit in this great air liner, as safe or safer
than we are at home in our armchairs, we should
take our hats off to the aerial pioneers, and particularly to those whose courage, whose perseverance and
whose technical skill are the foundation on which
Imperial Airways have built their wonderful services.

Among the organisations which assisted these early
flights an honourable place should be reserved for
that of the Shell Company, who soon realised the
importance of flying, and were always ready to
place at the disposal of experimenters the service of
their engineers and chemists.

IMPERIAL AIRWAYS

AND ASSOCIATED COMPANIES

A.H.A.OXFORD

VH-USE

10½ DAYS

AUSTRALIA

Right: This Imperial Airways poster from the mid-1930s could be described as a very simplified map, but the points of origin and destination of the journey are probably meant to be incidental to the main thrust and dynamism of the image emphasising both the speed and the implied safety and comfort of Imperial's four-engined De Havilland 86 aircraft. To reach Australia in only ten and a half days was a marvel in the 1930s, the only alternative being over a month by ship. The aircraft shown in the poster is actually registered to Qantas, the then Australian national airline, with which Imperial operated a joint service carrying the passengers to Singapore, then part of the British Empire, and transferring them to Qantas for the final part of the journey to Darwin and beyond. Ten and a half days is also a rather creative way of emphasising the speed of the journey – that was only the time it would take to reach Darwin. To go on to Brisbane or Sydney would take another one and a half or two and a half days respectively. (Brenet)

NEWEST, FASTEST AIRLINER IN THE WORLD!

B·O·A·C *Comet* JETLINER

G-BOAC

BRITISH OVERSEAS AIRWAYS CORPORATION

Left and opposite left: BOAC's poster headlined 'Newest, Fastest Airliner in the World!' above a cutaway image of the Comet 1 aircraft was certainly not an unsubstantiated advertising claim. Set above an image of the curvature of the earth and an outline of the southern hemisphere, the suggestion of height and speed that the map projects was entirely true. The Comet 1 was introduced in 1952 and as a jet aircraft, the very first commercial jet, immediately set new records, especially in speed. Flying at 490 mph as opposed to around 250 mph for propeller-driven aircraft, and much higher at around 35,000 feet, it slashed journey times, allowing Japan to be reached in thirty-six hours compared to the previous eighty-six hours (not least by eliminating two night stops). The Comet 1 gave a new meaning to the second BOAC poster, 'It's a small world by Speedbird', issued in the late 1940s. The cutaway image is of a Short Solent flying boat that had only started services to Japan in 1948, just four years before the Comet started service. The Solent service was almost obsolete before it started, not least because flying boats were rapidly being withdrawn as landplanes began to dominate the skies. The last of BOAC's flying boats stopped service in 1950. Where some artistic licence has been applied in the Comet 1 poster is in the depiction of the curvature of the earth. Even flying in Concorde nearly twenty five years later at 60,000 feet, the earth's curvature and darkness of the background of outer space was never seen quite like that!

Right: By the late 1920s, Imperial Airways was becoming a little more adventurous in its advertising. However, it still lacked the sort of excitement of the more innovative advertising created by Stuarts Agency, engaged as Imperial Airways' advertising agency in 1931. In this late 1920s advertisement a globe has been introduced, possibly for the first time, as Imperial's route network began to take on an intercontinental dimension as it expanded its network to the then British Empire, Egypt having been reached in 1925 and India in 1927. One would have thought that the artist would at least have marked Imperial's route network on the globe. Maybe something more subtle is going on and the large Union Flag in the background implies a dominion over much of the southern and eastern hemispheres of the globe so no need to highlight anything else?

This spread: Images of the aircraft used by Imperial Airways were important elements of their poster advertising in the 1920s and 1930s. This cutaway of a Short 'C' Class flying boat around 1937 clearly shows the close relationship to maritime terminology as well as highlighting the high degree of luxury and comfort that passengers could enjoy. Although aircraft had a clear speed advantage over shipping, especially on long-distance journeys, passengers expected the same or very similar levels of luxury and comfort that they enjoyed on board ship; airlines had to match that competition and advertise the fact. The aircraft's ability to take off and land on water is clearly shown, with a backdrop of somewhere in the eastern Mediterranean, probably Greece, as Imperial routed through Greek airspace on its way to Africa and the Far East. Imperial even had their own ship, *Imperia*, based in the Aegean to provide supplies to Imperial's flying boat services. The photograph shows a Short 'C' Class flying boat, possibly at Imperial's base at Southampton Water; apart from size, the similarities are very clear between the very traditional sailing ship and what was then the latest modern aircraft.

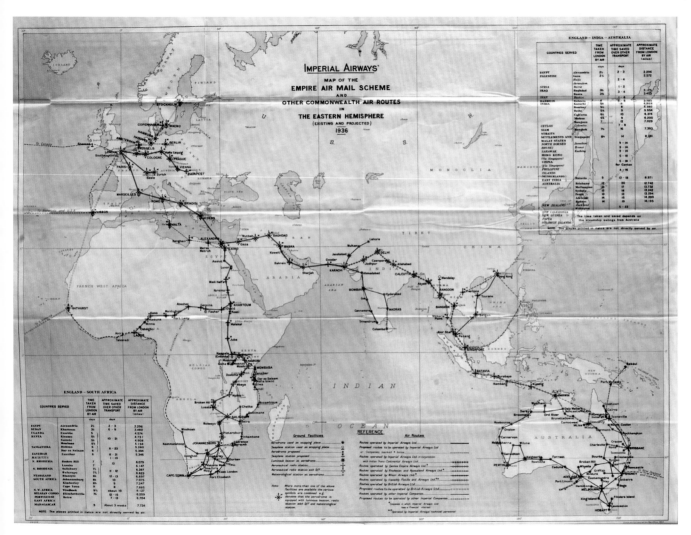

Although its exact purpose is unknown (it was probably used for internal information purposes following Imperial's introduction of the Empire airmail scheme), this world map, issued in 1937, provides a very useful summary of the extent of Imperial Airways' network and those of its associated companies. Drawn as a Mercator's projection (the standard projection for nautical charts where a ship's course could be shown as a straight line, as could an aircraft's), it became a widely used map projection for aviation. Other projections would also be used both for advertising and for navigation purposes dependent upon how best to depict (or imply) what was being shown.

This 1930s navigation chart for Southampton Water, issued in 1949 as a Gnomonic map projection, would be one of the last maritime charts to be used by BOAC as its last flying boat was withdrawn from service in 1950. BOAC was originally based at Hythe on the western side of Southampton Water following the end of the Second World War but later moved further into the main dock area to the Town Quay. Although difficult to read, the chart records where one of BOAC's Solent flying boats was forced to manoeuvre close to the western shore when the liner *Queen Elizabeth*, preparing to sail, moved off its designated path as tugs struggled to hold its position in a strong north-easterly wind. The reference to a 'collision' was not with the *Queen Elizabeth* but a buoy that was marking the aircraft marine taxiway – no serious damage was done to the aircraft or the buoy. (HMSO)

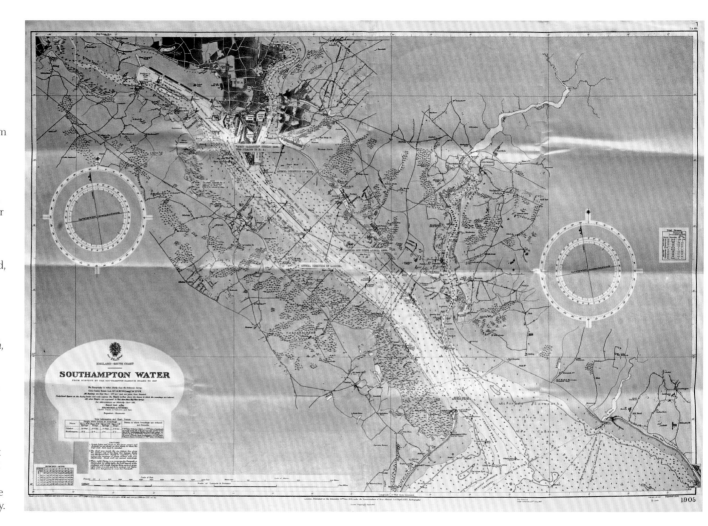

Left: By the mid-1930s, under the influence of Stuarts Agency, maps were often shown as a main feature in Imperial Airways' poster advertising. By this time Imperial's route network had expanded considerably as it carried out its remit to link Great Britain with what was then its empire. Highlighting that it operated the world's longest air route, the simplest and most striking way to show that was with a map – not a world map but one showing the southern and eastern continents, of which many countries were part of that empire. The western hemisphere would come much later; while the North Atlantic had been flown as early as 1919, it would not be until August 1939 that Imperial Airways operated its first service, and then only a mail service, between London and New York.

Opposite: In 1934 this striking world map poster was produced for Imperial Airways, probably by Stuarts Agency. A good example of an illustrated map showing all Imperial's services both European and intercontinental, it also includes Imperial's projected services to the USA and Canada that test flights, later carried out in 1937, would prove were viable. This poster raises the question of whether it falls within the classification of geography or art. It is probably somewhere in between, the map being the central feature and serving its purpose well in clearly highlighting the countries of the then British Empire and Imperial's routes. Imperial had been formed by the British government in 1924 principally to establish an Empire air route network and by 1934 it was well on the way to doing that, as the map clearly shows. The Mercator's projection used for the poster by its nature distorts the land areas of Canada and Australia in the northern and southern hemispheres respectively; this might be considered to imply a greater dominion over the surface of the planet than was actually the case, but it is unlikely this was intentional but merely a well-known effect of the map projection used. The map border artwork silhouettes are certainly works of art in themselves but they are supplementary to the main content that the map so graphically represents. Printed with reinforced eyelets so it could be easily hung, the poster was probably used principally in Imperial's offices and travel agencies as a ready reference guide. What the poster artworks also show are various aircraft silhouettes. These are not just there to highlight Imperial's fleet of aircraft but to show that different aircraft were to be used for different sectors of a journey. Flying from London to Cape Town would use four different aircraft types, including a flying boat to travel over the Mediterranean Sea, and would take five days.

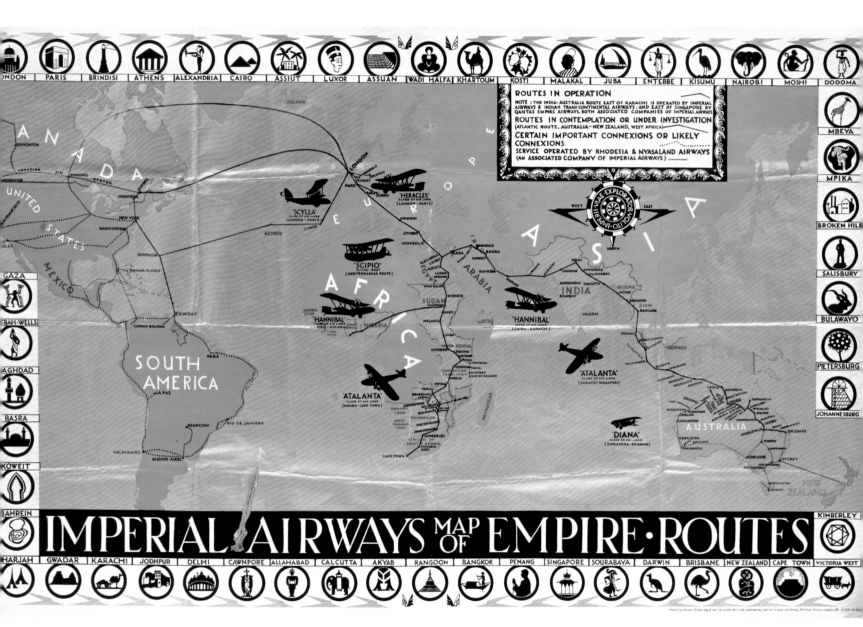

IMPERIAL AIRWAYS MAP OF EMPIRE·ROUTES

ROUTES IN OPERATION

NOTE : THE INDIA~AUSTRALIA ROUTE EAST OF KARACHI IS OPERATED BY IMPERIAL AIRWAYS & INDIAN TRANS-CONTINENTAL AIRWAYS : AND EAST OF SINGAPORE BY QANTAS EMPIRE AIRWAYS, BOTH ASSOCIATED COMPANIES OF IMPERIAL AIRWAYS

ROUTES IN CONTEMPLATION OR UNDER INVESTIGATION
(ATLANTIC ROUTE, AUSTRALIA~NEW ZEALAND, WEST AFRICA)

CERTAIN IMPORTANT CONNEXIONS OR LIKELY CONNEXIONS

SERVICE OPERATED BY RHODESIA & NYASALAND AIRWAYS
(AN ASSOCIATED COMPANY OF IMPERIAL AIRWAYS)

'SCYLLA'
CLASS OF AIR LINER
(LONDON ~ PARIS)

'HERACLES'
CLASS OF AIR LINER
(LONDON ~ PARIS)

'SCIPIO'
(FLYING ~ BOAT
(MEDITERRANEAN ROUTE)

'HANNIBAL'
CLASS OF AIR LINER
(CAIRO ~ KHARTOUM)

'HANNIBAL'
CLASS OF AIR LINER
(CAIRO ~ KARACHI)

'ATALANTA'
CLASS OF AIR LINER
(KISUMU ~ CAPE TOWN)

'ATALANTA'
CLASS OF AIR LINER
(KARACHI ~ SINGAPORE)

'DIANA'
CLASS OF AIR LINER
(SINGAPORE ~ BRISBANE)

CANADA
UNITED STATES
MEXICO
SOUTH AMERICA
EUROPE
AFRICA
ASIA
ARABIA
SUDAN
INDIA
BURMA
SIAM
AUSTRALIA
NEW ZEALAND

Top border cities: LONDON · PARIS · BRINDISI · ATHENS · ALEXANDRIA · CAIRO · ASSIUT · LUXOR · ASSUAN · WADI HALFA · KHARTOUM · KOSTI · MALAKAL · JUBA · ENTEBBE · KISUMU · NAIROBI · MOSHI · DODOMA

Right border cities: MBEYA · MPIKA · BROKEN HILL · SALISBURY · BULAWAYO · PIETERSBURG · JOHANNESBURG · KIMBERLEY

Bottom border cities: SHARJAH · GWADAR · KARACHI · JODHPUR · DELHI · CAWNPORE · ALLAHABAD · CALCUTTA · AKYAB · RANGOON · BANGKOK · PENANG · SINGAPORE · SOURABAYA · DARWIN · BRISBANE · NEW ZEALAND · CAPE TOWN · VICTORIA WEST

Left border cities: GAZA · BAH-WELLS · BAGHDAD · BASRA · KOWEIT · BAHREIN

Printed by Vincent Brooks Day & Son Ltd London W.C.1 and published by Imperial Airways Ltd, Airway Terminal, Victoria London S.W.1 14/138 300 5/36

2

GEOGRAPHY OR ART?

Almost inevitably, airline poster advertising follows the art and design trends and fashions of the time – sometimes exotic, sometimes contemporary or even almost simplistic, but generally, by their nature and purpose, eye-catching. In that sense they are artworks in themselves and the inclusion of a map, stylised or otherwise, becomes part of that work. There are many examples where there appears to be no question that we are dealing with art and not geography, but when a map or globe dominates the work does that not change the perspective? Maps can certainly influence one's perception, but when they are ancillary to the main subject they must be part of that artwork as a whole and serve what it seeks to represent or imply.

Harry Beck's well-known stylised route diagram of the London Underground is, in my view, both an artwork and a practical, broadly geographical representation, albeit not drawn as a geographically accurate map. As an example of modern design Beck's diagram is art, but it was not supposed to be; its primary purpose was to provide an easy guide to travel on the various lines of the London Underground and their interconnections. As a practical map it works very well and there are several similarly styled diagrammatic maps in the commercial aviation world, particularly from the 1930s and 1940s, possibly using Beck's idea as a general guide.

Following its start-up in 1924, Imperial Airways' early years were not marked by any real attempts to portray its advertising or general information for passengers as art but as mediums for getting information across and little else. These years were more about establishing Imperial's operations and planning to develop its route network; even passengers were secondary to that, with the carriage of mail taking precedence. With Imperial's successful General Post Office (GPO) bid for the carriage of mails it had a financial certainty, and advertising for passengers was very much second place, although passenger flights did provide an important revenue contribution. Imperial may have briefed its first advertising agency to focus on its route development rather than anything else and this may have accounted for the rather ordinary and not exactly inspiring early material. It would not be until the early 1930s that Imperial, now with a new and very forward-thinking publicity manager, Bill Snowden-Gamble, changed its advertising agency to Stuarts Agency, one of the up-and-coming London agencies with an eye for artistic talent, new styles and promotional ideas.

The use of Stuarts Agency transformed Imperial's advertising and its publicity material blossomed into a veritable cornucopia of art styles and themes. This was not art for the sake of art, however, but the beginning of a modern approach to creative publicity and design solutions in many forms. The use of established artists such as Ben Nicholson, Edward McKnight Kauffer and F. H. K. Henrion (and even my favourite landscape watercolourist, Rowland Hilder), along with a host of others both well known and new, introduced both art and geography into Imperial's rapidly developing business. With the intervention of the Second World War in the 1940s, the inevitable backward step in resources and materials turned into a flurry of new work in the 1950s and 1960s. Imperial Airways had gone and its nationalised UK airline successors, BOAC, BEA and BSAA used Stuarts Agency for a short while, but promotional activities and branding, certainly for BOAC, were now closely controlled by an internal design committee using artists such as F. H. K. Henrion as consultants. Geography continued to take a central place in this period, with maps widely used to promote and inform on both BOAC's and BEA's businesses. In effect, mapping the airways as a concept very much took off in this period, even more so than earlier years, with often quite detailed maps given away to passengers to highlight their journeys and to promote the airlines' services generally. Many airline maps in the 1950s and 1960s were like geography books themselves in their detail and coverage. Illustrative art, however, began to take second place to photographic and graphic art in the second half of the twentieth century; by the early 1970s, it is hard to find anything noteworthy.

Right: This is Imperial Airways' second route map from 1926, showing its international routes other than Paris. Only Paris, Brussels, Rotterdam, Amsterdam and Cologne were operated in those early days. These pioneer routes were the mainstay of Imperial's operations until new, multi-engine aircraft began to enter the fleet later in 1926/7 and would allow expansion to the south and east as part of Imperial's grand plan to reach the British Empire's overseas territories. This map also highlights the time benefits of flying by air – three and a half hours by air to Cologne or twenty hours by train and ship. It is definitely a geographical map, by any stretch of the imagination.

Overleaf, top right: As part of its luxury Silver Wing-branded service, introduced in 1927 between London and Paris, Imperial Airways offered passengers a small booklet of sequenced, two-dimensional maps showing the route between Croydon, then the main London airport, and Le Bourget airport in Paris. Shown as a straight black line, the booklet explains that at the aircraft's average operating speed of ninety miles an hour, each section of the map should take approximately fourteen minutes to cover. At an operating height of only a few thousand feet, in fine weather there were very good opportunities to follow landmarks along the way. All in all it was a pleasant, albeit noisy, way to while away the two and a half hours the flight would take.

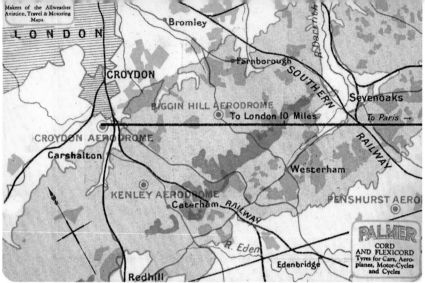

Left: Definitely a work of art. James Gardner's 1938 poster for Imperial Airways combines both art and geography. The general artwork takes centre stage and the stylised route diagram and globe provide a practical but secondary input while enhancing the overall effect. Gardner was one of the early commercial artists to use in aviation poster advertising a similar route diagram to that pioneered by Harry Beck in 1933 for his well-known London Underground route diagram map. Diagrammatic map content would become a common feature in aviation posters and information leaflets in succeeding years, not least because they provided both a pleasing and memorable impact as part of an advertisement but also gave practical information to a prospective traveller. Just like Beck's diagram, the geographical relationship between the named places listed bears no resemblance to reality, unlike a proper map indicating scale and distance, but served its purpose well, clearly indicating the route of travel and sequence of stops en route. (J. Gardner)

Opposite: Laszlo Moholy-Nagy may possibly have been the first artist to apply a Harry Beck-style route diagram as part of this 1936 poster advertisement for Imperial Airways. The predominant aspect is a world map and Moholy-Nagy even provides a key to 'The Map'. I'd call this geographical by any stretch of the imagination, but given Moholy-Nagy's pre-eminence as one of the leading influencers of early twentieth-century modernist abstract art, I hesitate to deny it is not (also) pure art. (Laszlo Moholy-Nagy)

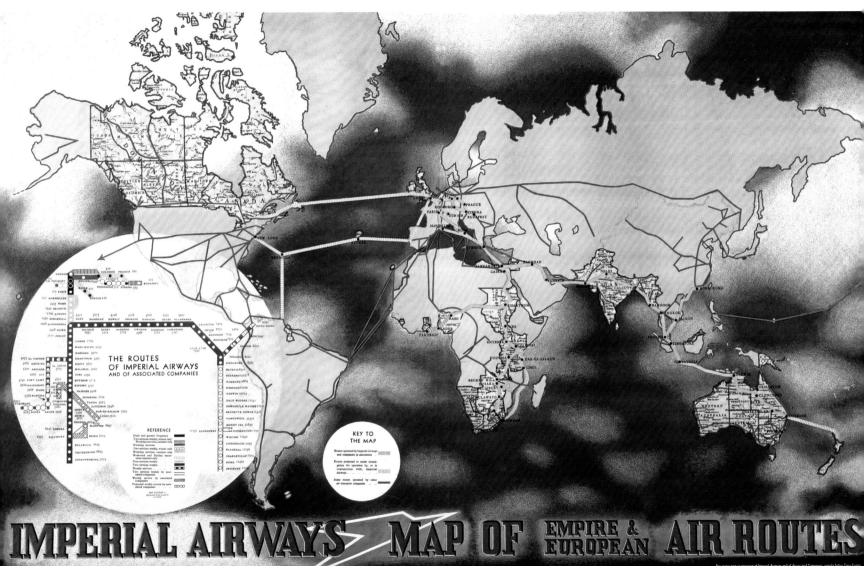

IMPERIAL AIRWAYS MAP OF EMPIRE & EUROPEAN AIR ROUTES

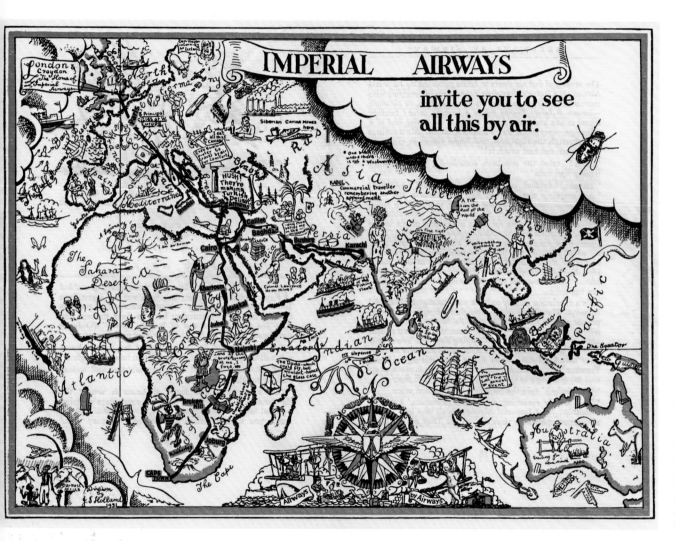

Commercial air travel in the 1920s and 1930s was very much a pioneering way to see the world, although by the early 1930s it had become well established and a viable, much quicker alternative to travel by ship for those who could afford it. With improvements in general education and geography very much a main focus in school curricula, the world was becoming a better-known place, at least from books, even to the general public. The locations and mysteries of far-flung places, especially those belonging to the British Empire, were of great interest to many people and maps were extensively used in printed matter as a very useful medium to educate and inform. Imperial Airways came to the same conclusion and, in 1931, produced this map as a centrefold in one of its promotional brochures, 'All Ways by Airways'. Solidly in the tradition of illustrated maps, this slightly tongue-in-cheek enticement to travel was entitled 'Imperial Airways invite you to see all this by air'. Who could fail to take up such an invitation? (J. S. Holland)

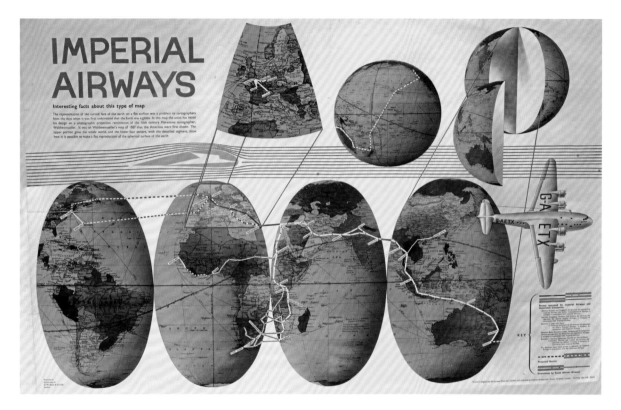

By 1938 Imperial Airways were really getting into their stride, using maps as part of their general advertising. Going way outside the traditional use of a Mercator map projection, the use of a more complex Waldseemueller projection was used to show how it was possible to make a flat reproduction of the spherical surface of the earth. Quite why Imperial believed this poster style would be of interest to prospective customers is not known. It may be to do with a wide general interest in maps by a public well used to seeing them and understanding what they reflected as representations of the British Empire. Imperial's advertising agency, Stuarts Agency, were also very creative, often pushing the boundaries of promotional art and using a wide range of well-known and innovative artists. The poster also provides 'interesting facts about this type of map', explaining that the poster artist (unnamed) has based his design on a photographic projection reminiscent of the sixteenth-century Florentine cartographer Waldseemueller; on his map of 1507 the Americas were first shown. This may provide a clue as to why Imperial used the projection. They had, a year earlier in 1937, completed trials proving the viability of a transatlantic operation to the USA and Canada (that began as a mail-only service in August 1939). Such a poster might therefore engage interest in the Americas as a new destination. (Stuarts Agency)

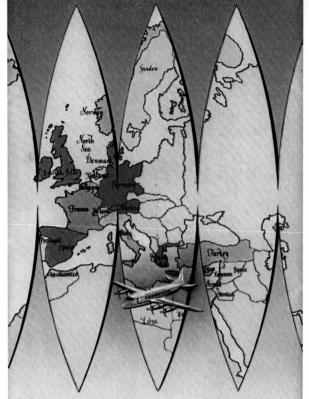

Making the world flat

There are many ways of making the world seem flat—of turning the globe into a map.

On every world map, air communications cross continents, countries and oceans. On many famous air routes, including those of B E A , the BP Aviation Service plays a vital part. Backed by the global resources of the Anglo-Iranian Oil Company, this Service provides the fuel for the B E A aircraft in which you fly.

RAIL AND AIR TRANSPORT•

Left: BOAC's sister company, BEA, was the second UK nationalised airline and was set up in 1946 to operate European routes to and from the UK. BEA also embraced the use of maps in its poster advertising, promotional and information material, including this brochure produced in cooperation with BP, who also used it to advertise its products. Interestingly, the brochure makes use of an illustration of 'gores', i.e printed sections of a world map cut out to use in the making of a globe, or, conversely, as the brochure states, 'There are many ways of making the world seem flat – of turning the globe into a map.' Quite why this type of illustration was used is unclear and it may have been that it neatly fitted the strapline of the advert rather than anything else more subtle. It is also hard to determine whether to call it art or geography, but it's probably a bit of both. It certainly makes an interesting and thought-provoking advert overlaid with a small image of a Vickers Viscount aircraft, one of BEA's principal aircraft during the 1950s. (BP)

Opposite right and right: Another example of pure art is this Imperial Airways brochure from the mid-1930s. Probably produced by Stuarts Agency, who were strong supporters of more modernist styles of graphic illustration, the image is of the front cover of a brochure promoting the carriage of parcels and freight jointly by the then four British railway groups (GWR, LMS, LNER and Southern) and Imperial Airways. McKnight Kauffer has incorporated a globe in his futuristic juxtaposition of aircraft and train silhouettes suggestive of speed and flight. Does the globe and backdrop of stars suggest a type of celestial geography or are they just indicative of the point of the brochure promotion, i.e. global travel? To ensure the latter point comes through the brochure conveniently also includes a much more standard, neatly illustrated map of Europe and Africa overlaid with Imperial Airways' route network. (Edward McKnight Kauffer)

Overleaf, spread: In 1940, Imperial Airways was merged with a private UK airline, British Airways Limited, and named British Overseas Airways Corporation (BOAC). BOAC flew throughout the Second World War under the control of the British Air Ministry, but in 1946, when civilian flying restarted, BOAC issued these diagrammatic route maps as part of its early promotional leaflets advertising its services. Very Harry Beck in style but going much further and incorporating a host of route symbols to indicate which of its services was operating a particular route, the maps are rather overcomplicated with a very detailed map legend and certainly not customer friendly from an interpretative perspective. These were early post-war years, however, and BOAC remained heavily influenced by its wartime operations, with the map reflecting almost Royal Air Force precision in its style and detail. BOAC appears to have appreciated that some may have found it overly stylistic and that 'geographical accuracy has been sacrificed for clarity and ease of handling', so they included a simple geographical map in a small box as a reference to where places really were. Even from a modernist perspective these maps cannot be considered art but appear unquestionably geographical, with an emphasis on place, representative location, links and all other unnecessary detail eliminated. It tells one broadly what goes where and nothing else, not unlike a modern aviator's navigation chart, albeit they were for a very different audience.

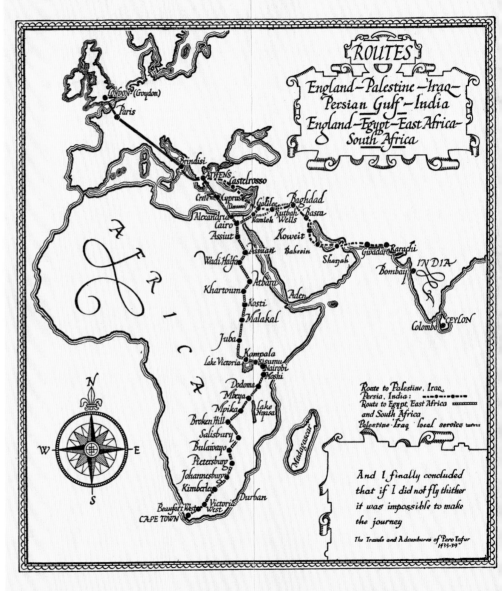

Printed in Great Britain by the Curwen Press, North St., E.
Published by Imperial Airways Ltd., London

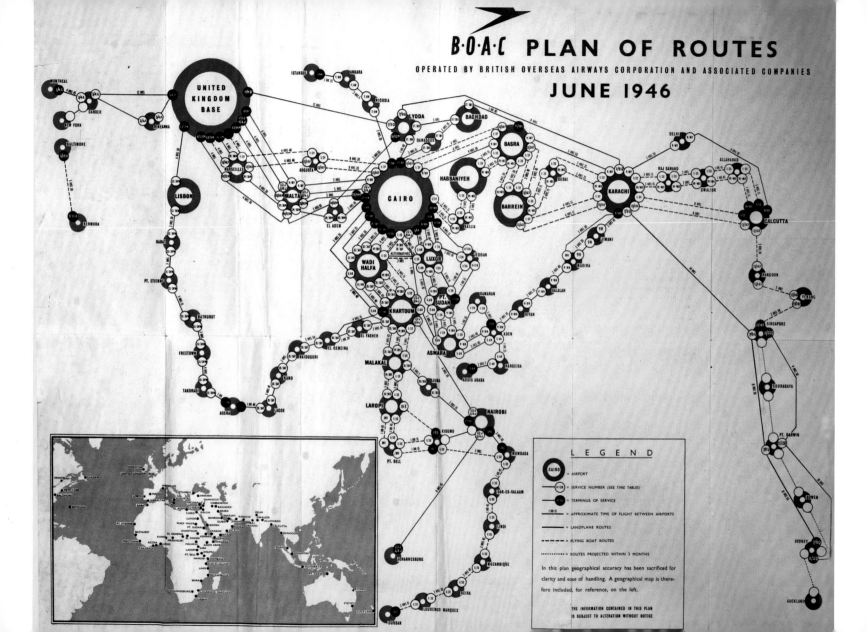

B·O·A·C PLAN OF ROUTES

OPERATED BY BRITISH OVERSEAS AIRWAYS CORPORATION AND ASSOCIATED COMPANIES

JUNE 1946

L E G E N D

- **AIRPORT**
- **SERVICE NUMBER** *(SEE TIME TABLES)*
- **TERMINUS OF SERVICE**
- **APPROXIMATE TIME OF FLIGHT BETWEEN AIRPORTS**
- **LANDPLANE ROUTES**
- **FLYING BOAT ROUTES**
- **ROUTES PROJECTED WITHIN 3 MONTHS**

In this plan geographical accuracy has been sacrificed for clarity and ease of handling. A geographical map is therefore included, for reference, on the left.

THE INFORMATION CONTAINED IN THIS PLAN IS SUBJECT TO ALTERATION WITHOUT NOTICE

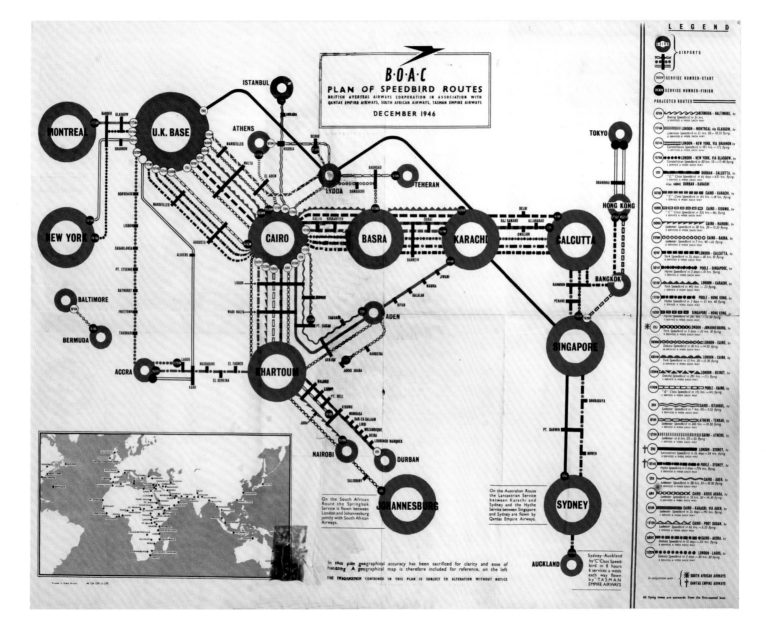

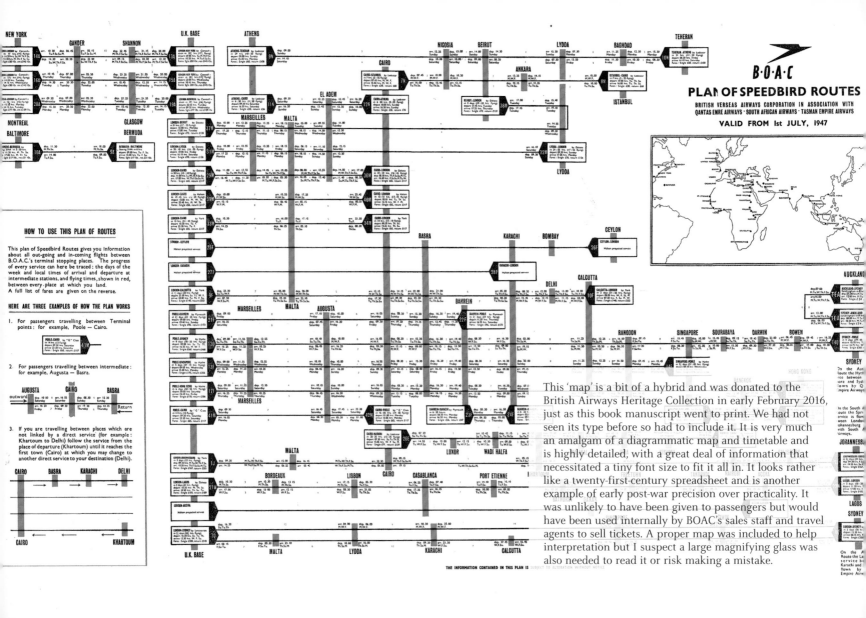

This 'map' is a bit of a hybrid and was donated to the British Airways Heritage Collection in early February 2016, just as this book manuscript went to print. We had not seen its type before so had to include it. It is very much an amalgam of a diagrammatic map and timetable and is highly detailed, with a great deal of information that necessitated a tiny font size to fit it all in. It looks rather like a twenty-first-century spreadsheet and is another example of early post-war precision over practicality. It was unlikely to have been given to passengers but would have been used internally by BOAC's sales staff and travel agents to sell tickets. A proper map was included to help interpretation but I suspect a large magnifying glass was also needed to read it or risk making a mistake.

Concurrent with its 1946 diagrammatic maps, BOAC also issued a more traditional route map for its services from the UK to the Middle East, India and Australia. This is definitely a map. It looks like a map and feels like a map drawn as a quite attractive three-dimensional image with simple graphics to denote seas, oceans and mountainous areas. Using what looks like a Bonne's projection, it has allowed the journeys to be shown broadly as straight lines on a minimum paper size. The map is interesting as it emphasises some of the very long sectors flown to Australia. Given the aircraft of the time this looks surprising, but these early services were flown by Avro Lancastrians, the civilian version of the famous wartime Lancaster bombers that were up to operating many hours in flight. Quite whether the passengers were also up to it is not known, and the long sectors must have been fairly gruelling – the first flight from the UK to Australia in May 1946 took sixty-three hours – but these early services were very much about communications, getting to Australia and back as quickly as possible as the British Empire sought to return to peacetime normality. While an attractive map, it is again not very passenger-friendly, with symbols and codes not easily interpreted. Even with a map legend, it still has a military feel about it.

3

FROM LANDMARKS TO WAY MARKERS

In the early days of commercial aviation, finding the way was often effected by the visual identification of prominent landmarks, compass bearings, road maps rested on knees and a lot of experience; not much different to walking the hills of southern England, but much faster and any mistakes could be a lot more serious! Railway lines with the names of their stations conveniently painted on their roofs were widely used as convenient tracks to follow and worked well in fine weather. Aircraft stayed on the ground at night in the absence of any form of radio aid or beacon, and even in daylight commercial pilots preferred to fly under the clouds rather than above them. Experience counted for a great deal both in flying the rudimentary aircraft of the day and knowing the route to follow.

The English Channel provided a daunting and potentially dangerous obstacle, but in fine weather the coast of France could be easily seen from a few thousand feet up in the air. The route was very well known, having been flown thousands of times during the First World War. Many of the commercial pilots had themselves been in combat during that war, so they were well used to flying in adverse conditions. However, they now had fare-paying passengers to consider, so safety and keeping on schedule were of primary importance. Once the Channel had been flown it was due south along the French coastline until Le Touquet, then inland on a compass bearing of 160 degrees, keeping the railway line to starboard until Abbeville and on to Beauvais, and then Paris. Large-scale road maps were often widely used in the early days of aviation until specific aeronautical maps were developed in later years.

As the nationalised airline of Great Britain, Imperial Airways worked closely with the Royal Air Force (RAF) in establishing its route network. The RAF were themselves true pathfinders as they spread their wings overseas in protection of British interests abroad. Imperial Airways would quickly follow as it began its journey to establish commercial aviation links with the countries of the British Empire, India being of particular interest as the empire's so-called 'jewel in the crown'. Egypt was a key destination as a hub from which to develop Imperial's empire routes, especially those to India via the Arabian Gulf and southwards to East Africa and the Cape. Great Britain also had major interests in the Gulf area, and the RAF had surveyed and mapped the principal route as early as 1921. This provided a valuable template which Imperial could use to develop its bases and establish refuelling stops across what was invariably a very harsh desert environment; in effect, the RAF explored and set out the ground markers that Imperial's pilots could follow across an often featureless terrain.

It was soon realised that following maps devised for road traffic was not the most effective way to navigate an aircraft, even when they flew at under 100 miles per hour. Much of the detail of most UK Ordnance Survey maps was also unnecessary for aviators, but features of prominence would stay – railways lines remained, as did large buildings and rivers, coastlines and towns and cities, easy to recognise and use as points of reference. Contours and high points were also retained as particularly important features for rather obvious reasons, but airfields and airports were mapped in more detail to guide pilots when taking off and landing. Radio aids for direction finding and identification were also developing fast during the 1930s, as was air-to-air and air-to-ground communication. Mapping the airways from a navigational perspective was beginning to take on the broad shape of, and provide the foundation for, the mapping systems of the later twentieth century.

In 1937, less than twenty years after AT&T's first scheduled passenger flight, an experimental crossing of the North Atlantic between Foynes in the then Irish Free State and Botwood in Newfoundland, Canada, by an Imperial Airways flying boat proved that the route could be flown as a commercial service. There would, however, be no following of railways lines or markers across deserts, let alone relying on sighting any prominent natural features such as rivers and coastlines, except at each end of the route. The bit in between, the North Atlantic Ocean, was a much more daunting prospect than the English Channel had been in 1919; it would be featureless as far as the eye could see and accurate navigation would be critical. The weather would be critical, too. In fact, accurate meteorology reports were just as important as finding the right course. The North Atlantic, especially in winter, is notorious for its bad weather, with strong winds, snow and ice and severe operating conditions generally, especially for the aircraft of the time, which would often have had to fly *through* the weather rather than *above* it. Get it wrong and the aircraft could ice up, potentially with disastrous results.

Two years of meteorological data was recorded in order to gauge the likely conditions and best months to operate. Finding the way would be by a combination of celestial sightings, 'shooting the sun and stars' to find a bearing and calculating distance flown, a form of 'dead reckoning' navigation using maritime charts and radio support from the many commercial ships plying the route; their slower progress across the ocean allowed accurate courses to be plotted that could be cross-referenced with the aircraft overhead and any corrections made to keep it on course. The relationship of the maritime and flying worlds were never closer than on those experimental flights and would remain so for several years until more sophisticated and longer-range radio and beacon navigational aides were developed during the Second World War.

Accurate navigation using charts and the stars was even more critical during the Second World War. British Overseas Airways Corporation (BOAC) began regular weekly services between Great Britain and the USA/Canada flying westbound and eastbound all year, the very first time the North Atlantic had been flown in both the summer and winter. There were no ships with which to check course bearings, especially at night running with no lights and in complete darkness and with a radio communications blackout. BOAC also continued to operate to Africa and around the Indian Ocean to India and Australia, often using Imperial's large old flying boats on long circuitous routings far out into the mid-Atlantic to avoid occupied Europe and the Mediterranean; navigators were almost as important as pilots on these long and hazardous journeys. Their skill in finding the way using the night sky as a chart to calculate a bearing and the route to follow cannot be underestimated.

Direction-finding systems continued their rapid development following the ending of the Second World War in 1945. Aviation-specific maps had also become well established during the war, with the old strip-type maps superseded by detailed sectional charts for lower altitudes and airport-specific maps (which showed topography, identifiable physical features, beacons and radio frequencies) and world aeronautical charts detailing high altitude routes, the motorways of the sky if you like. Even for a pilot, the detail of these maps takes some getting used to, but, just like Ordnance Survey maps, once you know the scales and conventional signs they become comfortable old friends in finding the way.

Roll on to the twenty-first century – while physical maps are still retained in some commercial aircraft cockpits, just in case, computers have taken on the task of plotting the way. Pressing a button or flicking a switch is far easier for modern pilots than wrestling with a large paper document and mathematical calculations, although not so interesting. In many modern commercial aircraft in recent years GPS now rules the skies and, in a way, takes us full circle to those early days. Direction finding by GPS has become a commonplace for many motorists and aviators just as road maps used to be. Fortunately for aviators, and the rest of us, incidents of getting lost are few and far between, although that can't be said of some motorists.

A rather dirty and oil-stained French road map from the early 1920s, sold by the British cartographic company Edward Stanford, bound in what looks like the early twentieth-century equivalent of duct tape. It was used by one of Handley Page's pilots, who had marked his way in red ink to highlight the route from Paris to Zurich. Handley Page was a predecessor airline of British Airways, being one of four British airlines who were bought in 1924 by the British government to form Imperial Airways. The map is a good example of the make-do-and-mend approach to aviation direction finding in its early years. Key features such as railways lines and railway stations have been marked by pencilled squares where they crossed the air route. If the pilot misinterpreted the terrain, a fixed rail line or station could keep him on track. The only practical maps of any accuracy for aviators at this time were those produced for terrestrial use and were either bought from mapmakers direct or simply from a high-street bookshop.

From the mid-1930s Imperial Airways flew the stately Handley Page HP42 aircraft on the overland part of the route to India via either Gaza in what was then British Palestine or Cairo in Egypt. This picture is at Rutbah Wells in Iraq. The Arabian Desert was a mixture of sand, rock and sometimes sharp stone surfaces, but the dominant feature was its vastness, often featureless as far as the eye could see. The RAF's mapping and identification markers were critical in finding a safe route across this dangerous area and identifying safe places to land.

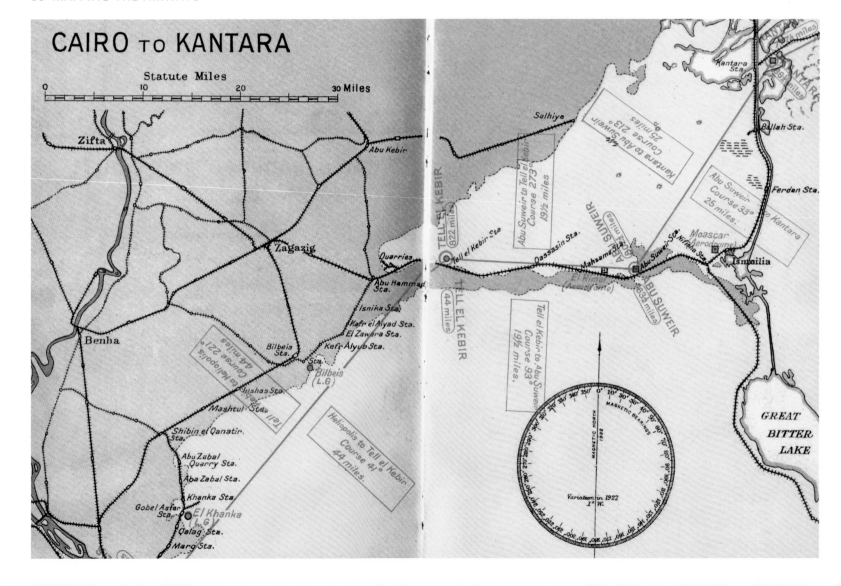

CAIRO TO KANTARA

Statute Miles

This spread: These maps, issued in 1926, show two sections of the desert airmail route between Cairo and Baghdad. The route was first used by the Royal Air Force and then taken over by Imperial Airways when it commenced its first services from Cairo to Baghdad as a first step towards developing its Empire route linking Great Britain to India. The maps are highly detailed and for several sectors are referred to by the names of the places at each end of the sector concerned, e.g. Cairo to Kantara. In areas where there were no places, the route was designated alphabetically eastbound up to El Jid and then in Roman numerals eastbound to Ramadi. It is not clear quite why this was done other than to facilitate locating an aircraft should it have to make a forced landing. With the extremely hot and dry weather conditions along the route, there was a real fear for the safety of aircrew and passengers should they not be found and rescued quickly. (HMSO)

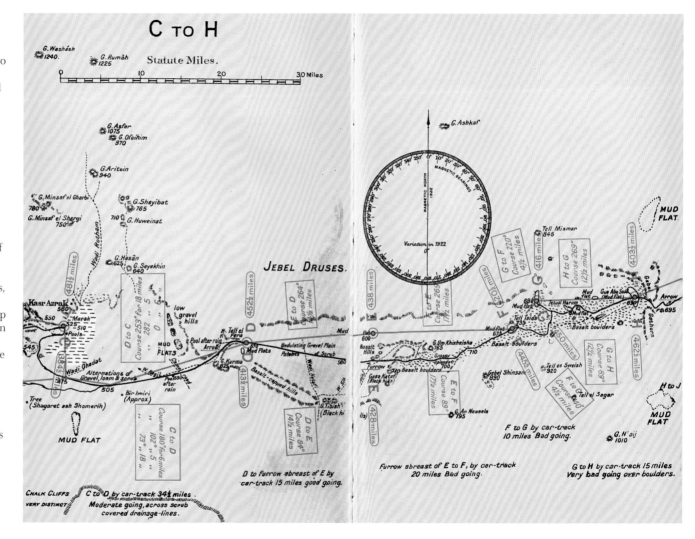

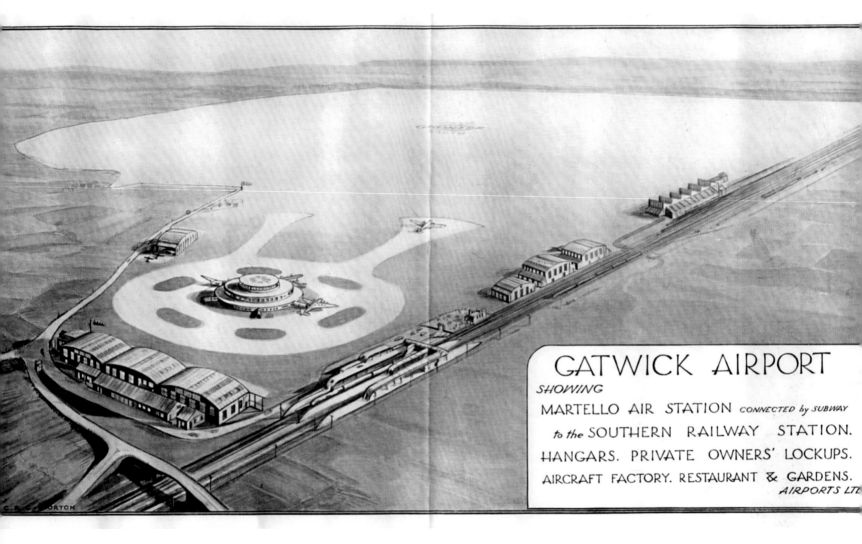

GATWICK AIRPORT
SHOWING
MARTELLO AIR STATION CONNECTED by SUBWAY
to the SOUTHERN RAILWAY STATION.
HANGARS. PRIVATE OWNERS' LOCKUPS.
AIRCRAFT FACTORY. RESTAURANT & GARDENS.
AIRPORTS LTD

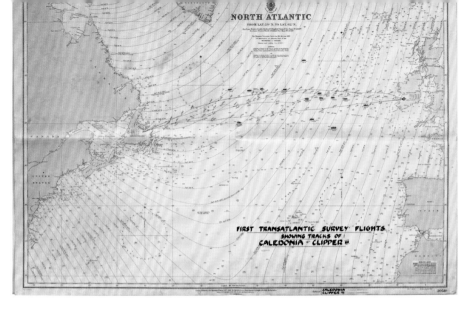

First transatlantic survey flights showing tracks of *Caledonia - Clipper III*

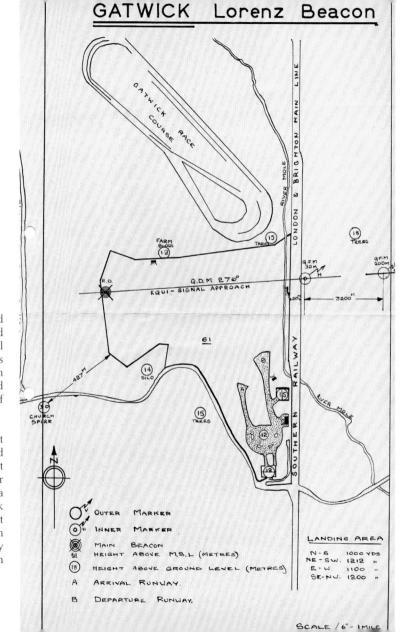

GATWICK Lorenz Beacon

GATWICK RACE COURSE

RIVER MOLE

LONDON & BRIGHTON MAIN LINE

Q.D.M. 276° EQUI-SIGNAL APPROACH

SOUTHERN RAILWAY

LANDING AREA
N-S   1000 YDS
NE-SW 1212 "
E-W   1100 "
SE-NW 1200 "

⊙ OUTER MARKER
◉ INNER MARKER
⊛ MAIN BEACON
51 HEIGHT ABOVE M.S.L (METRES)
(18) HEIGHT ABOVE GROUND LEVEL (METRES)
A ARRIVAL RUNWAY.
B DEPARTURE RUNWAY.

SCALE 6" = 1 MILE

Opposite and right: This rather crude hand-drawn map of Gatwick's airfield was prepared by Imperial Airways for its pilots in the later 1930s. The important link between the airfield and the London to Brighton railway line is very clear, with Gatwick's then new terminal (nicknamed 'the Beehive') directly connected to the railway station. The airfield beacon was located on a bearing of 276 degrees, with aircraft landing primarily in a westerly direction into the prevailing wind. Being a grass airfield, however, other landing directions could be made dependent upon the wind direction, but pilots needed care to take account of obstacles such as trees and buildings. (Opposite: C&C Morton)

Above and overleaf: This chart was carried on the Imperial Airways 'C' Class flying boat *Caledonia* on 5 July 1937 when it flew from Foynes in the then Irish Free State to Botwood in Newfoundland, Canada, then on to Montreal and New York. While the flight proved that commercial services could be made across the North Atlantic, it was also a test of the weather forecast for that day, based on the previous two years of meteorological data, and was a complete success. The navigation was a complete success, too. The aircraft's navigator took a rhumb-line bearing (a straight line on the chart and a slightly longer course than a great circle one) using sun and star sightings and 'dead reckoning' corroborated by bearings given by many ships crossing the Atlantic that day. The ships, carefully drawn on the chart as they were overflown, would have been using the same charts as the aircraft's navigator, Squadron Leader Godsave, seen here plotting a course on a later flight in September 1937.

Opposite left: The Canadian Pacific liner *Empress of Britain* departing the St Lawrence River in July 1937 – the liner was one of those ships that provided valuable navigation assistance to Imperial Airways' *Caledonia* on its first Atlantic crossing. The *Empress of Britain* was the largest and fastest ship of her time but was lost to enemy action just three years later at the beginning of the Second World War.

Opposite right: Believe it or not, this is the high-altitude radio navigation chart over western Europe for 1978. It looks very complex but is really just a motorway in the sky, albeit rather a spaghetti junction in places. Going west, just keep on the UR8 to Land's End. (British Airways)

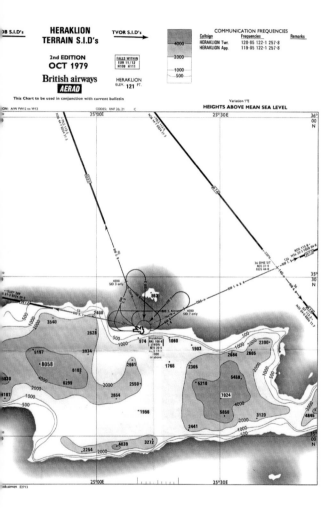

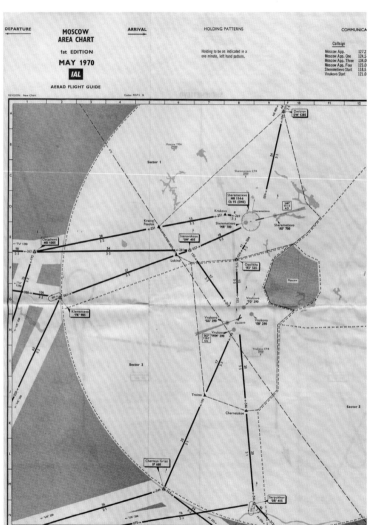

At lower altitudes a lot less detail is recorded but what is recorded is just as critical as these 1970s maps imply. The map of Heraklion airport in Greece clearly shows the high ground to the south of the airport, an area clearly to be avoided, hence the approach and take-off over open sea. Further north in Europe, but restricted not by terrain but by government regulation, the airspace around Moscow's main airports was severely limited due to numerous military no-fly areas, due to the USSR's wish to control overflying during the 'Cold War'. Crossings between western and eastern European air corridors were just as strictly controlled as on the ground; get it wrong at the Russian end and a MiG fighter would very quickly turn up. (British Airways)

ALL HEIGHTS IN FEET ABOVE MEAN SEA LEVEL

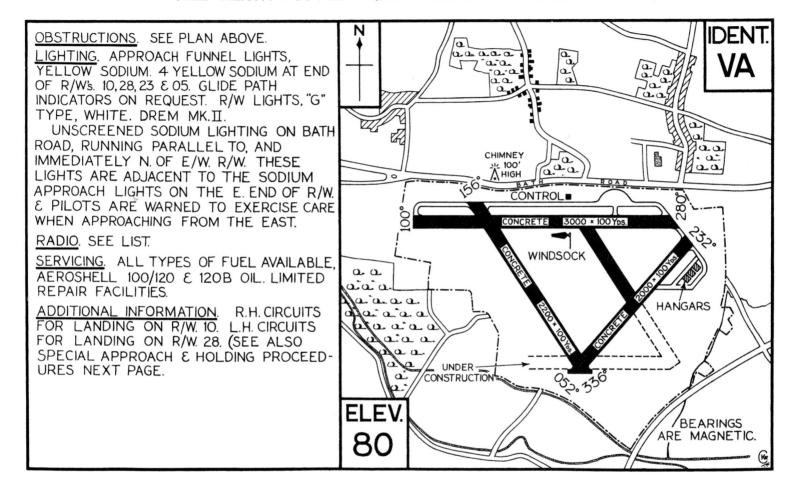

OBSTRUCTIONS. SEE PLAN ABOVE.

LIGHTING. APPROACH FUNNEL LIGHTS, YELLOW SODIUM. 4 YELLOW SODIUM AT END OF R/W's. 10, 28, 23 & 05. GLIDE PATH INDICATORS ON REQUEST. R/W LIGHTS, "G" TYPE, WHITE. DREM MK. II.

UNSCREENED SODIUM LIGHTING ON BATH ROAD, RUNNING PARALLEL TO, AND IMMEDIATELY N. OF E/W. R/W. THESE LIGHTS ARE ADJACENT TO THE SODIUM APPROACH LIGHTS ON THE E. END OF R/W. & PILOTS ARE WARNED TO EXERCISE CARE WHEN APPROACHING FROM THE EAST.

RADIO. SEE LIST.

SERVICING. ALL TYPES OF FUEL AVAILABLE, AEROSHELL 100/120 & 120B OIL. LIMITED REPAIR FACILITIES.

ADDITIONAL INFORMATION. R.H. CIRCUITS FOR LANDING ON R/W. 10. L.H. CIRCUITS FOR LANDING ON R/W. 28. (SEE ALSO SPECIAL APPROACH & HOLDING PROCEEDURES NEXT PAGE.

IDENT. VA

N

CHIMNEY 100' HIGH

156° 280° 232°

100°

CONTROL

CONCRETE 3000 × 100 YDS.

WINDSOCK

CONCRETE

2200 × 100 Yds.

2000 × 100 Yds.

HANGARS

CONCRETE

UNDER CONSTRUCTION

052° 336°

BEARINGS ARE MAGNETIC.

ELEV. 80

This London airport airfield map used by BEA's pilots in October 1947 is almost unrecognisable compared to today. Opened in May 1946, only the northern runway and two cross-runways were completed by then, with the southern runway still under construction even in late 1947. There were no terminal facilities at all and the first one would not open until seven years later in what became Central Area in the middle of the airfield. Even the control tower was still outside the centre, alongside the A4 Bath Road, close to where passengers checked in, first in tents and later in prefabricated buildings.

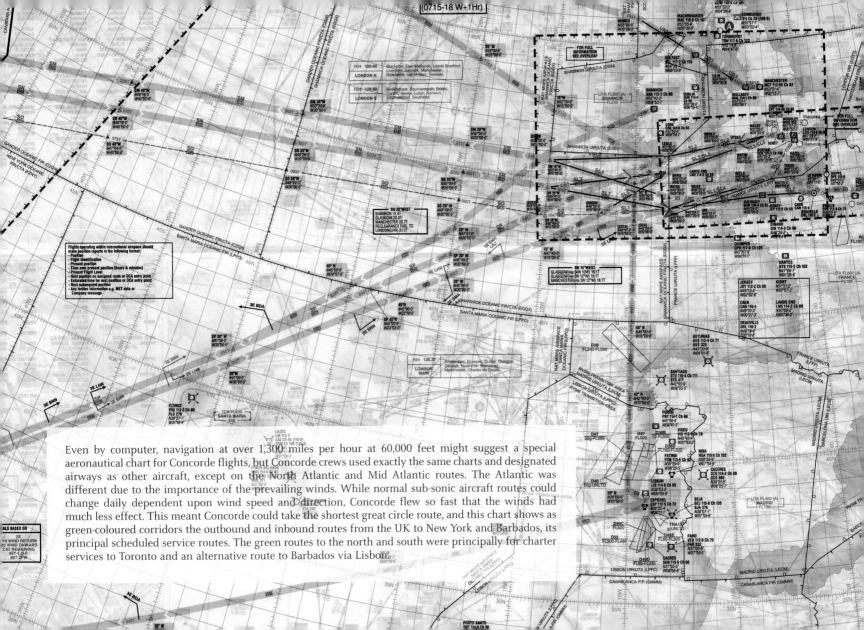

Even by computer, navigation at over 1,300 miles per hour at 60,000 feet might suggest a special aeronautical chart for Concorde flights, but Concorde crews used exactly the same charts and designated airways as other aircraft, except on the North Atlantic and Mid Atlantic routes. The Atlantic was different due to the importance of the prevailing winds. While normal sub-sonic aircraft routes could change daily dependent upon wind speed and direction, Concorde flew so fast that the winds had much less effect. This meant Concorde could take the shortest great circle route, and this chart shows as green-coloured corridors the outbound and inbound routes from the UK to New York and Barbados, its principal scheduled service routes. The green routes to the north and south were principally for charter services to Toronto and an alternative route to Barbados via Lisbon.

The approach to Hong Kong's old Kai Tak airport was always 'interesting', especially at low level in the typhoon season, when flying between the apartment blocks and lines of washing as Kai Tak was inside the city boundary alongside the harbour. This airport map appears almost home-made and may have been used as a pilot's training aid. Ground heights are clearly marked, very important given the hilly terrain. At the 'KL' beacon, identified both by instrument readings (ILS) and a loud voiceover calling the turn, prominent chequerboard hoardings were also placed on the ground as a not-to-be-missed visual reminder to pilots to turn right for the final approach. Behind the boards a mountain and some large apartment buildings loomed, so they were not to be ignored! The boards can be clearly seen in this late 1990s photograph of a British Airways B747 on final approach to Kai Tak. Having turned at the chequerboard hoardings, the aircraft's pilot, Captain Simon Scholey, has made the turn to 135 degrees to line up with the runway. The aircraft is painted in British Airways 1997 'World Images' livery, with the Kalahari Desert design on its tailfin by the artist Cg'ose Ntcox'o of the Ncoakhoe tribe of the San people of the Kalahari Desert.

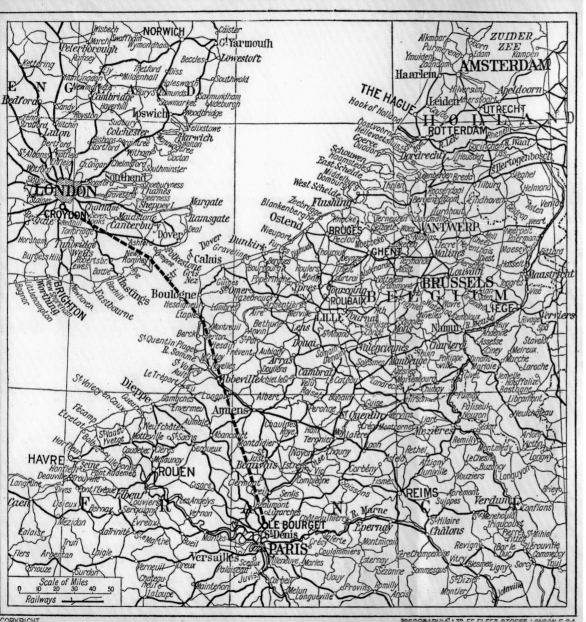

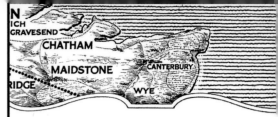

London to Paris on "BP

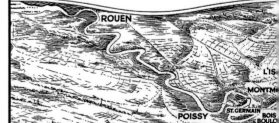

ONE HUNDRED YEARS OF SHOWING THE WAY

This chapter brings us to the main event, the cornucopia of art styles and themes mentioned in the second chapter. One hundred years is itself a bit of artistic licence, as British Airways has not quite made its century – 25 August 2019 will mark that event – but it is a neat chapter title and sums up the long span of time during which maps have been a central feature of the airline's promotion, information and operation. Unfortunately, very little map material survives from the first five years of this story, but that disappointment is rapidly compensated for as the 1920s progress and the 1930s blossom; no legend is necessary for their interpretation or conventional signs to identify their features. Each image speaks for itself, but an explanatory note is included where necessary or appropriate.

This spread: A rather bland start is this very simple map that was stitched into a Handley Page booklet entitled 'By Air', produced for passengers on its London (Croydon) to Paris (Le Bourget) services in the very early 1920s. The simplicity of the map is surprising and was clearly considered secondary to the very informative travelogues included for each section of the route, including good-quality photography of sights that would be overflown. A much more interesting inclusion in the booklet is a BP advertisement for its 'BP' aviation spirit, which was used to fuel Handley Page's aircraft engines, highlighting its 'purity, uniformity, and high quality'. BP used as a backdrop a quite nice three-dimensional map, albeit much of it is hidden by the advert. A very similar map was subsequently used in its entirety by Imperial Airways as one of its early advertising posters following its takeover of Handley Page in 1924; see chapter 1. (Opposite right: BP; right: Geographia Ltd)

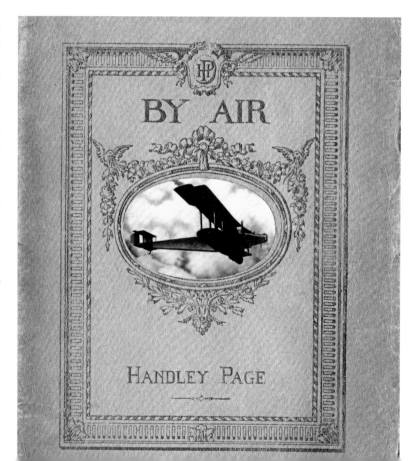

INSTONE LONDON-PARIS AIR SERVICE

THE INSTONE AIR LINE, managed by Messrs. S. Instone & Co., Ltd., the well-known firm of steamship and colliery owners, is backed by a powerful and well-tried organisation with exceptional practical knowledge of transportation problems. The managers of the Instone Air Line have special, and considerable, first-hand experience of the London-Paris air route, on which they have operated, almost continuously, ever since commercial flying between London and Paris became a real and business-like proposition.

Messrs. Instone employ Vickers-Vimy and D.H.18 aeroplanes, the passenger-carrying portions of which form well-ventilated limousine saloons, in which each passenger is allotted a comfortably upholstered arm-chair, with ample space for freedom of movement. The saloons are fitted with sliding triplex glass windows, and each passenger has a continuous view of the regions flown over. Luggage compartments and lavatory accommodation are provided in the rear portions of the saloon.

During flight the Instone Air Line machines are in continuous touch with the ground organisations by means of wireless telegraphy and telephony. Passengers require no special clothing.

TYPES OF MACHINES USED.—(i) **Vickers-Vimy** twin-biplane, with two 375 H.P. Rolls-Royce motors. Seating accommodation : 11 passengers. Carrying capacity : 2620 lb. of commercial load. (ii) **D.H.18** single-tractor biplane, with one 450 H.P. Napier motor. Seating accommodation : 8 passengers. Carrying capacity: 1800 lb. of commercial load.

CONVEYANCE OF PASSENGERS TO AERODROME.—London passengers for Paris are conveyed free by motor car, which leaves daily from the New Metropole Hotel, Northumberland Avenue, at 11.00 o'clock. (See also daily press announcements.) Paris passengers for London are conveyed free to the Le Bourget Air Port by motor car, which starts daily from 1 Rue des Italiens at 11.00 o'clock.

Map illustrating the Instone Air Route.

PARCELS AND GOODS : LONDON-PARIS RATES.—Goods are accepted subject to the conditions printed on the back of the Company's consignment notes, a copy of which must be signed by the sender of every parcel.

*For Parcels up to £2 in declared value** (including collection in London and delivery in Paris) :

Up to 1 lb.	...	1/6	Up to 8 lb.	...	4/-	Up to 15 lb.	...	6/2
,, 2 ,,	...	1/10	,, 9 ,,	...	4/2	,, 16 ,,	...	6/6
,, 3 ,,	...	2/9	,, 10 ,,	...	4/4	,, 17 ,,	...	6/10
,, 4 ,,	...	3/-	,, 11 ,,	...	4/6	,, 18 ,,	...	7/2
,, 5 ,,	...	3/3	,, 12 ,,	...	4/11	,, 19 ,,	...	7/6
,, 6 ,,	...	3/6	,, 13 ,,	...	5/4	,, 20 ,,	...	7/10
,, 7 ,,	...	3/9	,, 14 ,,	...	5/9	For each additional lb., 5d. per lb.

Reduced Rates for large or regular consignments.

Light and bulky parcels are subject to increased rate according to bulk.

FORMALITIES.—All parcels must be accompanied by (i) Consignment Notes completely filled in ; (ii) Customs Declaration Form No. 901, giving exact quantities, size and weight of the articles in the parcel ; (iii) Invoice showing the value of each article in the parcel.

PARCELS AND GOODS : PARIS-LONDON RATES.

Up to 10 kg.	4.50 fcs. per kg.	From 20-40 kg.	4.00 fcs. per kg.	From 60-100 kg.	3.00 fcs. per kg.
From 10-20 kg.	4.25 ,,	,, 40-50 kg.	3.75 ,,	,, 100-500 kg.	2.50 ,,

LATEST TIMES OF DESPATCH FROM LONDON to arrive in Paris on the afternoon of the same day :—

9.15	SELFRIDGE & CO., LTD., Oxford Street.	9.45	T. MEADOWS & CO., 35 Milk Street.	10.12	
9.20	CARTER, PATERSON & CO., 6 Maddox Street.	9.47	THOS. COOK & SON, 70 Cowcross Street.	10.15	H. JOHNSON & SONS, 18 Byward Street.
9.30	INSTONE AIR LINE, 3 Kingly Street.	10.10	BECK & POLLITZER, 135 Queen Victoria St.	10.30	INSTONE AIR LINE, 53 Leadenhall Street.

LATEST TIMES OF DESPATCH FROM PARIS : 9.30, M. NOIZET, Faubourg du Temple ; 9.45, AIR EXPRESS CO., 25 Rue Royale ; 9.55, COX'S SHIPPING AGENCY, 15 Boulevard de la Madeleine ; 10.00, INSTONE AIR LINE, 1 Rue des Italiens ; 10.25, Messrs. JOHNSON.

* Parcels exceeding £2 in value (insured separately by the consignor) may be sent under these rates, but the Company will not be liable beyond the value of £2 unless the consignor makes a written declaration of the value of such goods and, previously to carriage, pays the agreed increased rate of charge for such carriage

Left: This page is from an April 1922 promotional brochure advertising the services of the Instone Air Line, one of the predecessor companies of Imperial Airways, including a very simple map. Not much more was needed as Instone only operated between London (Croydon airport) and Paris (Le Bourget). What is more surprising is the wealth of information about the service generally, even in these very early days of air travel. Everything had been carefully thought through to ensure as complete and trouble-free a journey as possible for Instone's passengers.

Opposite: Imperial Airways' first timetable was issued in early 1925 for its summer operations. This was a very comprehensive booklet on Imperial's services, but with a rather basic centrefold map taken for reuse from another Imperial Airways brochure, 'By Air to Anywhere', a commendably thrifty approach at a time when costs were high and passengers few in number. The map suggested, at first glance, that Imperial had a wide network of northern European services. In fact, Imperial only operated a few direct services from London's Croydon airport, with connections by other European airlines or by rail. Overland, railways were the airlines' major competitors given the high cost of air fares, and this would remain the case for several decades for the vast majority of the travelling public.

MAP OF EUROPEAN AIR ROUTES

British Air Lines shewn thus ——
Other do do do - - -
Night Train Service do — — —

Imperial Airways Limited

By Air to Anywhere

Imperial Airways
Limited.

SEMPER SECVRVS

:: SUMMER ::
TIME TABLES
and Freight Rates

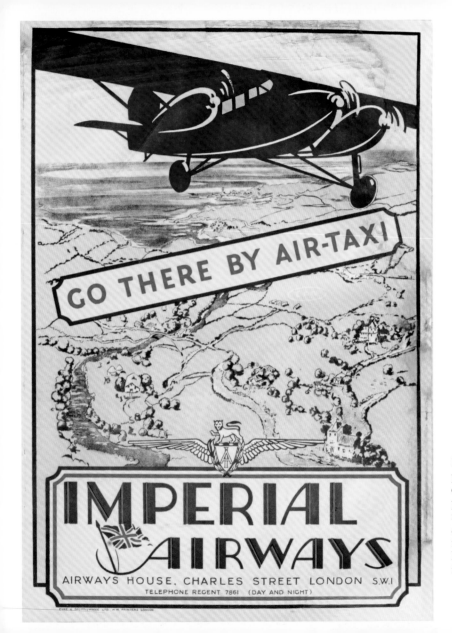

In the late 1920s, Imperial Airways offered their own air taxi and private hire service within Britain and across Europe. These were some of the earliest private air services and the forerunner of the extensive private charter business that operates today. Accompanying promotional material tells us that 'all Imperial Airways aeroplanes are totally enclosed, adequately ventilated and BRITISH' and can be hired for 2s a mile (£6.38 in 2015). It is an interesting but unimpressive poster and one of the last before Imperial changed its advertising company to the much more innovative Stuarts Agency in 1931.

A map of Imperial's early route that commenced in 1929 to Karachi (then in British India) and flew from Cairo to Baghdad and Basra then routed over the northern side of the Persian Gulf via Bushire and Bundar Abbas. The map is perhaps a forerunner of change, reflecting the waning influence of British overseas power and its empire, a trend that would accelerate following the Second World War. The Persians blocked the continuation of the northern routing in 1932, forcing the British government to negotiate with several of the southern Gulf kingdoms to allow services via the southern side of the Gulf. India itself would also be given its independence in August 1947 and Karachi would become the first capital city of Pakistan.

CAIRO - BAGHDAD - KARACHI -
AIR SERVICE.

IMPERIAL AIRWAYS LTD

MAP OF ROUTE

A BRITISH SERVICE

Only British machines and engines are used on this service. All machines on this service have three engines and are capable of flying on two. All have lavatory accommodation.

PILOTS

All pilots are British with brilliant records and long flying experience and are fully licenced by the British Air Ministry.

ENGINEERS

Each machine carries a qualified engineer licenced by the British Air Ministry.

WIRELESS

Each machine carries wireless apparatus and maintains communication with the various Air Ports.

WEIGHT

British aeroplanes are never overloaded. Every item of load is weighed prior to departure to ensure that the total load is within the permissible limit.

IMPERIAL AIRWAYS LTD.
Air Port of London,
CROYDON, SURREY.

'Phone :
CROYDON 2046

'Grams :
"FLYING, CROYDON."

And at
CAIRO, GAZA,
BAGHDAD and
BASRA.

'Grams :
" AIRWAYS "

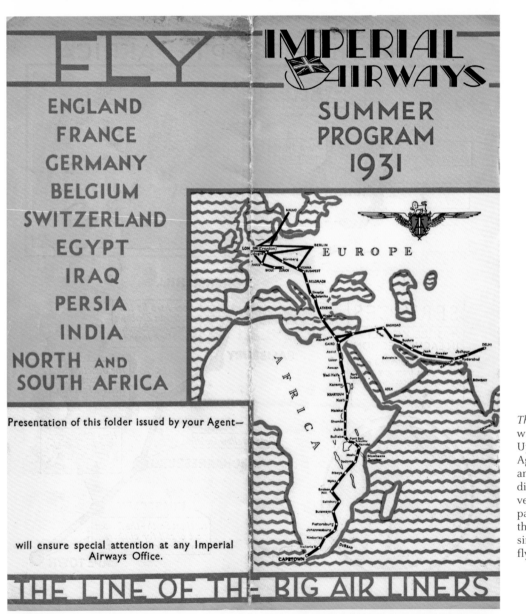

FLY IMPERIAL AIRWAYS

SUMMER PROGRAM 1931

ENGLAND
FRANCE
GERMANY
BELGIUM
SWITZERLAND
EGYPT
IRAQ
PERSIA
INDIA
NORTH AND SOUTH AFRICA

Presentation of this folder issued by your Agent—

will ensure special attention at any Imperial Airways Office.

THE LINE OF THE BIG AIR LINERS

This spread: Imperial Airways continued to use maps widely in its timetables to illustrate its route network. Up to 1931 and before the engagement of Stuarts Agency, they were still quite basic. They also included an embryonic version of route maps, in this case a diagrammatic one that would, in later years, become very detailed and highly illustrated giveaways to passengers. The photographs, however, broadly stayed the same. Why pay another photographer to take a similar shot of the Arch of Ctesiphon or Imperial's flying boats at anchor in Mirabella Bay, Crete?

IMPERIAL AIRWAYS

TIME TABLE
EUROPEAN DIVISION

WINTER SERVICES - 1929—19[??]

ENGLAND — EGYPT — INDIA

LONDON — Here all Airways Start —

ATHENS — A Pageant of the Past

CRETE

"The Isles of Greece where burning Sappho loved and sung"

"Here in the Quiet Hills." Imperial Airways beautiful Mediterranean Base at Mirabella, Crete, showing two flying-boats on the England-India service and the depot ship "Imperia."

ALEXANDRIA — Where seafaring men of all Nations meet

CAIRO

The Nile, the Pyramids and the Setting Sun

GAZA — Gateway to the Holy Land

SERVICES
ONCE WEEKLY IN EACH DIRECTION

Full time-tables and rates on request from any travel agency, or direct from the Company.

BAGHDAD

Jewel of the East

Sinbad's home, port for dates, oil and carpets.

BASRA

Here Persia's treasures go to sea

BUSHIRE

KARACHI — Junction for all India

Town built on an Eagle's Nest

JODHPUR

Between Baghdad and Basra, on the India route, the world-famed Arch of Ctesiphon

Noble Capital of a mighty country

DELHI

One of Stuarts Agency's first creative offerings for Imperial Airways was this wraparound cover for its 1931/32 winter timetable. The artistry is particularly eye-catching, the vibrancy of the image of a Handley Page HP42 aircraft over a stylistic depiction of Imperial's route network being in marked contrast to the rather bland imagery of earlier years. Timetables suddenly became miniature works of art and not just a collection of flight numbers and schedules – decorative and informative at the same time. (J. S. Holland)

By the summer of 1932 Imperial's timetable illustrations continued their upward climb in style and decoration. Who better than Edward McKnight Kauffer to provide another flourish for Stuarts Agency, including for the first time Imperial's brand new logo, called the 'Speedbird', designed by Theyre Lee-Elliott earlier that year. (Edward McKnight Kauffer)

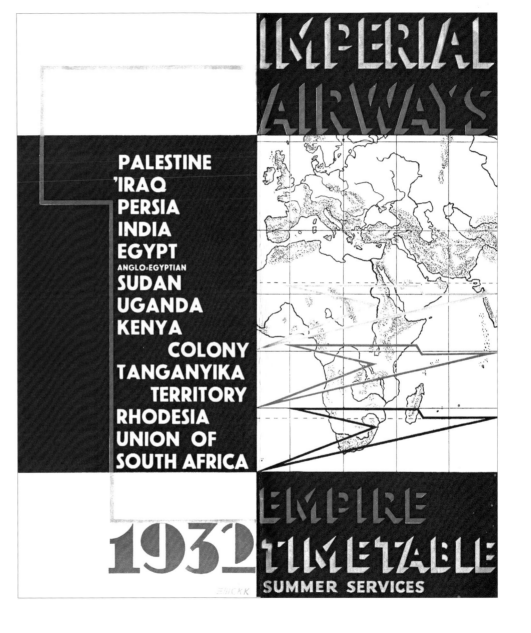

IMPERIAL AIRWAYS

PALESTINE
'IRAQ
PERSIA
INDIA
EGYPT
ANGLO-EGYPTIAN
SUDAN
UGANDA
KENYA
COLONY
TANGANYIKA
TERRITORY
RHODESIA
UNION OF
SOUTH AFRICA

1932 EMPIRE TIMETABLE
SUMMER SERVICES

This spread: The Speedbird logo became Imperial Airways' brand mark and had considerable longevity for over fifty years, being adopted first by BOAC in 1940 and later in 1974 by British Airways. It was widely used during the 1930s to illustrate, decorate and identify Imperial's services in many forms of advertising, information and other paper documentation. The 'England to India in 7 days' poster, issued in March 1932, is probably the first time it was ever used in advertising. Conversely, the 'Fly to India in 3 days' poster, issued in August 1939, is probably the last time it was used, as civilian flying ceased less than four weeks later following the start of the Second World War on 3 September. The Speedbird logo was not used on aircraft until 1939 as Imperial's management took the view it was not appropriate to decorate its rather austere aircraft livery of pale grey with a stylistic symbol. (This page and overleaf: Theyre Lee-Elliott)

GO TO THE
GRAND NATIONAL
BY
AIR
£8 - 8s.
RETURN
IMPERIAL AIRWAYS
THE BRITISH AIR LINE

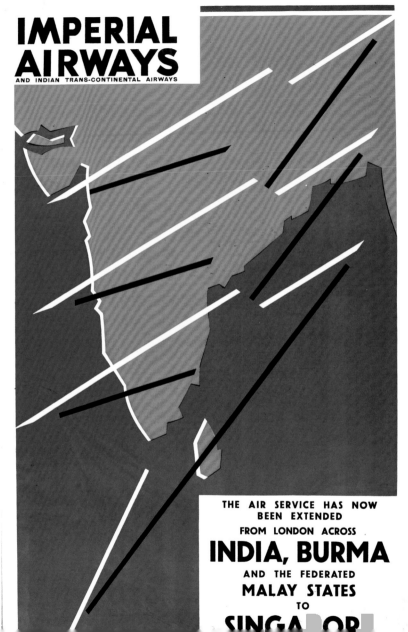

IMPERIAL
AIRWAYS
AND INDIAN TRANS-CONTINENTAL AIRWAYS

THE AIR SERVICE HAS NOW
BEEN EXTENDED
FROM LONDON ACROSS
INDIA, BURMA
AND THE FEDERATED
MALAY STATES
TO
SINGAPORE

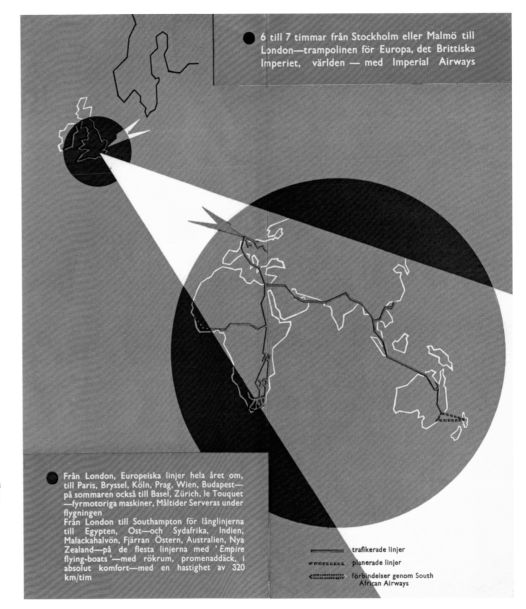

6 till 7 timmar från Stockholm eller Malmö till London—trampolinen för Europa, det Brittiska Imperiet, världen — med Imperial Airways

This page and overleaf left: Eager to make use of the new brand mark, Stuarts Agency took the opportunity to place the Speedbird firmly in the public eye and put it on almost anything and everything that promoted Imperial's services. Route maps and timetables were an obvious choice and, in time, like any good brand mark, it became recognised as Imperial Airways, with the company name in small print or even omitted entirely. (Stuarts Agency)

Från London, Europeiska linjer hela året om, till Paris, Bryssel, Köln, Prag, Wien, Budapest— på sommaren också till Basel, Zürich, le Touquet —fyrmotoriga maskiner, Måltider Serveras under flygningen
Från London till Southampton för långlinjerna till Egypten, Ost—och Sydafrika, Indien, Malackahalvön, Fjärran Östern, Australien, Nya Zealand—på de flesta linjerna med 'Empire flying-boats '—med rökrum, promenaddäck, i absolut komfort—med en hastighet av 320 km/tim

———— trafikerade linjer

ⱤⱤⱤⱤⱤⱤⱤ planerade linjer

⟨⟨⟨⟨⟨⟨⟨⟨ förbindelser genom South African Airways

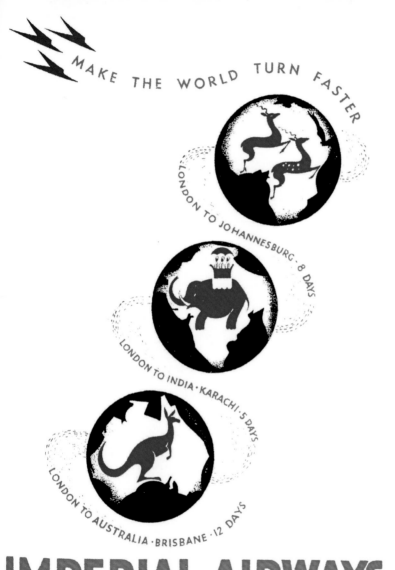

MAKE THE WORLD TURN FASTER

LONDON TO JOHANNESBURG · 8 DAYS

LONDON TO INDIA · KARACHI · 5 DAYS

LONDON TO AUSTRALIA · BRISBANE · 12 DAYS

IMPERIAL AIRWAYS

THE EMPIRE'S AIRWAY

Above, opposite and overleaf: Imperial Airways produced many information leaflets and brochures and, from time to time, more comprehensive booklets lavishly illustrated by prominent artists. 'The Empire's Airway' was one example, with designs and photography by Laszlo Moholy-Nagy, one of the twentieth century's pioneers of modernist abstract art. Maps and globes in association with the Speedbird symbol made an appropriate setting for Moholy-Nagy's interpretation, which makes simply the point that Imperial spanned the empire and in time would span the world. (Laszlo Moholy-Nagy)

EUROPE'S BIGGEST AIR-LINER
THE IMPERIAL *ENSIGN*

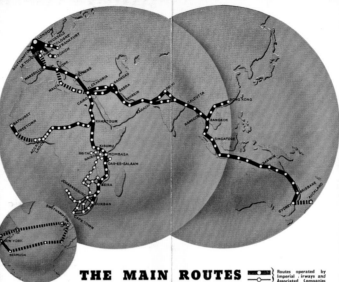

THE MAIN ROUTES

OF IMPERIAL AIRWAYS

Routes operated by Imperial Airways and Associated Companies

Projected routes

Connexions by South African Airways System

The World's Greatest Air Comfort

Every one of Imperial Airways' fleet of over 75 big air-liners has four engines for security—the only air company in the world to insist upon this safeguard

❦ they are all so effectively sound-proofed that you can talk as comfortably as in an express train

❦ the adjustable chairs are the most comfortable on land or sea or air—adjustable from sit-up to lie-back positions without your having to get up

❦ on the main routes the air-liners have smoking cabins and promenades

❦ you have one, or sometimes two, stewards to look after you—bring you drinks at any time or answer any questions

❦ there is ample toilet accommodation on board

❦ on most routes you can have meals as you fly

❦ there is plenty of room for luggage and a generous amount of luggage is carried free

THE IMPERIAL FLYING-BOAT · THE ENSIGN & FROBISHER AIR-LINERS

AIR MAIL

By the use of the air mail, letters can now be sent, and a reply received, in less time than is needed just to send a letter by the fastest alternative means.

So great, are the advantages of air mail that the British Government has decided as a matter of principle that in the future letter mails within the British Empire will, so far as is practicable, be carried by air.

The weight of letter mails carried by air from this country for the quarter ending 30 September 1935 has increased by 76 per cent. as compared with the corresponding quarter of 1934.

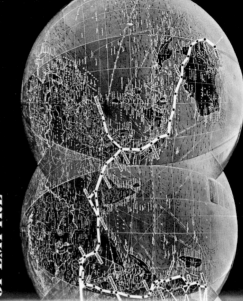

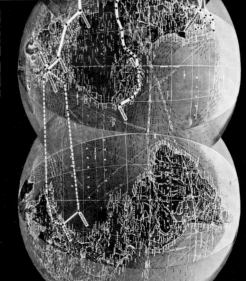

THE LINK OF EMPIRE

Routes operated by Imperial Airways and Associated companies

Projected routes

Connexion by other Air Lines

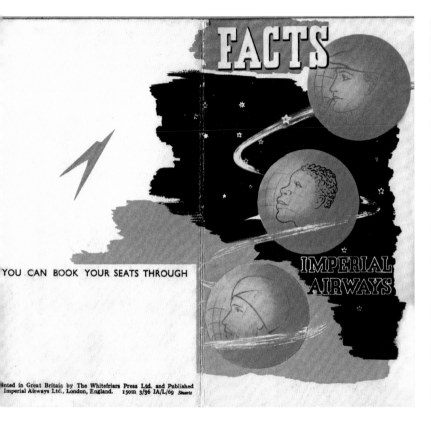

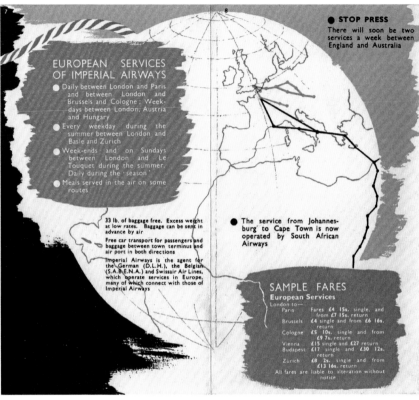

This spread: Moholy-Nagy also produced other designs for Imperial Airways' publicity, including this information leaflet that uses the subtle imagery of three globes on its front cover with ethnic images reflective of Imperial's spanning of both European and empire air routes. (Laszlo Moholy-Nagy)

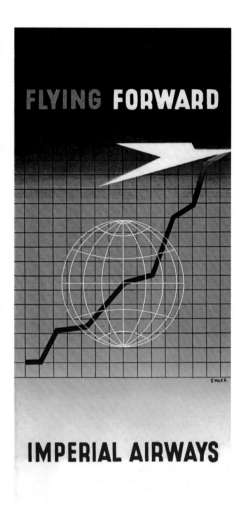

FLYING FORWARD

IMPERIAL AIRWAYS

Mr. G.E. Woods Humphery C.B.E.

Far left: McKnight Kauffer also produced information leaflets for Imperial Airways. This very simple graphic design from the later 1930s, overlaid by a diagrammatic zig-zag route over an outline of a globe, does not need any message. The title, 'Flying Forward', says it all. Although they operated a number of what were becoming obsolete aircraft, Imperial were part of a rapidly evolving modern world in which air travel was seen as a leading component. (Edward McKnight Kauffer)

Left: Even more subtle is Moholy-Nagy's use of a splash of paint and a silhouette of a flying boat and letter over a globe. The document was the cover of a presentation by Imperial Airways MD of the time, G. E. Woods Humphery, so the image did not need its own message or brand mark association that would have been appropriate for a wider audience. The image did, however, clearly bring together the association between Imperial Airways and the GPO's Empire Airmail Scheme, which was now operative across the world outside of the Americas. (Laszlo Moholy-Nagy)

Continuing the modernist style, Stuarts Agency engaged Edward McKnight Kauffer and Ben Nicholson to produce these eye-catching posters from around the mid-1930s. Both have simple messages but draw the eye with their strong, graphical presentation. While McKnight Kauffer uses a traditional world globe overlain by Imperial's route network, Nicholson is more abstract, with an Oriental-style depiction of what I presume is the earth (or is it the sun? A globe, anyway) and bold Speedbirds linking both globe and message. (Right: Edward McKnight Kauffer; Far right: Ben Nicholson)

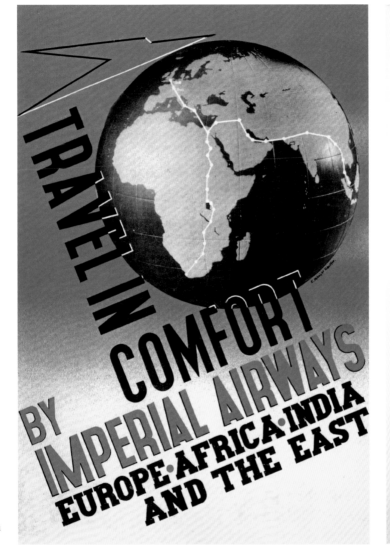

FLY THROUGH EUROPE

ENGLAND, FRANCE, BELGIUM, GERMANY, SWITZERLAND, CENTRAL EUROPE.

IMPERIAL AIRWAYS

FLY EUROPE

FLY

IMPERIAL AIRWAYS

This spread, next three pages: Imperial Airways was often criticised for not developing a wider European network, an unfair criticism as its principal remit was to open up routes to the British Empire. Its European route promotional literature could often be quite plain and simple – factual without any frills. However, Imperial did try to encourage travel to the few European cities it did serve, either direct or in conjunction with other airlines, with many an eye-catching image and coloured maps on a variety of promotional documents.

Details of the European services of Imperial Airways and of air transport companies for which it acts as agents are given in *Imperial Airways European Services* timetable. Obtainable from any office of the Company and from its Agents

AGENT

Printed in England by Charles & Read, Ltd., and Published by Imperial Airways, Ltd., London, England
IA/L/262 50m 5/38

Stuarts

FLY TO EUROPE

By Imperial Airways

SEE EUROPE BY AIR WITH SPEED AND COMFORT

LIVERPOOL
COPENHAGEN
MALMÖ
FLENSBURG
KIEL
LÜBECK
HAMBURG
DANZIG
BREMEN
LONDON
PLYMOUTH
LeZOUTE
Amsterdam
Rotterdam
BERLIN
POSEN
SOUTHAMPTON
Essen
DORTMUND
LEIPZIG
BRESLAU
CHERBOURG
Ostend
Antwerp
DÜSSELDORF
DRESDEN
GLEIWITZ
Le Havre
Brussels
Cologne
FRANKFORT
PRAGUE
PARIS
MANNHEIM
NÜRNBURG
ORLEANS
BASLE
MÜNICH
TOULOUSE
ZÜRICH
MARSEILLES
FLORENCE
TRIESTE
CANNES
TURIN
VENICE

A.E. TAYLOR. 33

ASK THE PURSER FOR ILLUSTRATED BOOKLETS & TIMETABLES

BY **air** TO
CENTRAL EUROPE IN LESS THAN A DAY

IMPERIAL AIRWAYS
S·A·B·E·N·A

DAYS TO SOUTH AFRICA
2 BRINDISI · ATHENS
3 CAIRO · WADI HALFA · KHARTOUM
4 JUBA
5 ENTEBBE · KISUMU · NAIROBI
6 DODOMA · M'BEYA
7 BROKEN HILL
8 SALISBURY · BULAWAYO · JOHANNESBURG
DAYS TO WEST AFRICA
4 EL OBEID · EL FASHER · GENEINA
5 ABESHER · ATI · FORT LAMY · MAIDUGARI · KANO

DAYS TO AUSTRALIA
2 BRINDISI · ATHENS
3 GAZA · BAGHDAD
4 BASRA · KOWEIT · BAHREIN · SHARJAH
5 GWADAR · KARACHI · JODHPUR
6 DELHI · CAWNPORE · ALLAHABAD · CALCUTTA
7 AKYAB · RANGOON · BANGKOK
8 PENANG · SINGAPORE
9 BATAVIA · SOURABAYA · RAMBANG
10 KOEPANG · DARWIN
11 LONGREACH
12 CHARLEVILLE · BRISBANE
DAYS TO CHINA
9 TOURANE
10 HONG KONG

TRAVEL THROUGH
EUROPE BY AIR

Europe is covered with a vast network of air lines. You can fly between all the big cities, saving time and money
Ask your travel agent or Imperial Airways how you can use the European air services to your best advantage

EUROPEAN SERVICES
OF IMPERIAL AIRWAYS

★ Daily between London and Paris. Every weekday between London and Brussels and Cologne ★ Weekdays between London and Germany, Czechoslovakia, Austria and Hungary ★ There is a night air mail every weekday to Berlin ★ Every weekday during the summer between London and Basle and Zürich ★ Week-ends and on Sundays between London and Le Touquet during the summer ★ Meals served in the air on most routes

33 lb. of baggage free. Excess weight at low rates. Baggage can be sent in advance by air. Free car transport for passengers and baggage between town terminus and air port in both directions ★ *Imperial Airways is the General Agent for the German (D.L.H.), the Belgian (S.A.B.E.N.A.) and Swissair Lines, which operate services in Europe, many of which connect with those of Imperial Airways*

For full details of services mentioned in this book, see Imperial Airways Timetables, obtainable from any office of the company or travel agents. Business people will find *Bradshaw's International Air Guide*, published monthly, price 1s. from any newsagent in the United Kingdom, of use, as it gives full details of air services

SAMPLE FARES

LONDON TO

PARIS	Fares £4 15s. single and from £7 15s. return
BRUSSELS	£4 single and from £6 16s. return
COLOGNE	£5 10s. single and from £9 7s. return
VIENNA	£15 single and £27 return
BUDAPEST	£17 single and £30 12s. return
ZÜRICH	£8 2s. single and from £13 16s. return

All fares are liable to alteration without notice

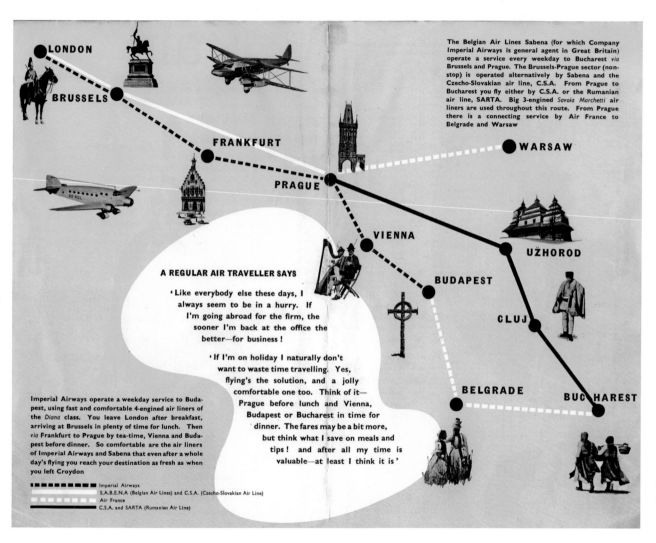

The Belgian Air Lines Sabena (for which Company Imperial Airways is general agent in Great Britain) operate a service every weekday to Bucharest via Brussels and Prague. The Brussels-Prague sector (non-stop) is operated alternatively by Sabena and the Czecho-Slovakian air line, C.S.A. From Prague to Bucharest you fly either by C.S.A. or the Rumanian air line, SARTA. Big 3-engined *Savoia Marchetti* air liners are used throughout this route. From Prague there is a connecting service by Air France to Belgrade and Warsaw

A REGULAR AIR TRAVELLER SAYS

'Like everybody else these days, I always seem to be in a hurry. If I'm going abroad for the firm, the sooner I'm back at the office the better—for business!

'If I'm on holiday I naturally don't want to waste time travelling. Yes, flying's the solution, and a jolly comfortable one too. Think of it—Prague before lunch and Vienna, Budapest or Bucharest in time for dinner. The fares may be a bit more, but think what I save on meals and tips! and after all my time is valuable—at least I think it is '

Imperial Airways operate a weekday service to Budapest, using fast and comfortable 4-engined air liners of the *Diana* class. You leave London after breakfast, arriving at Brussels in plenty of time for lunch. Then via Frankfurt to Prague by tea-time, Vienna and Budapest before dinner. So comfortable are the air liners of Imperial Airways and Sabena that even after a whole day's flying you reach your destination as fresh as when you left Croydon

▪▪▪▪▪▪▪▪▪ Imperial Airways
░░░░░░░░ S.A.B.E.N.A (Belgian Air Lines) and C.S.A. (Czecho-Slovakian Air Line)
━━━━━━ Air France
━━━━━━ C.S.A. and SARTA (Rumanian Air Line)

Opposite, next two spreads: One European country Imperial Airways did make a strong promotional effort on was Switzerland. As a destination for skiing and mountain walking, there was a significant demand to fly there. It could be reached in only half a day, allowing the weekend ski break to become a reality. The country's rugged terrain called for a variety of three-dimensional stylised images and maps to draw in prospective customers. (Opposite, far left: Theyre Lee-Elliott)

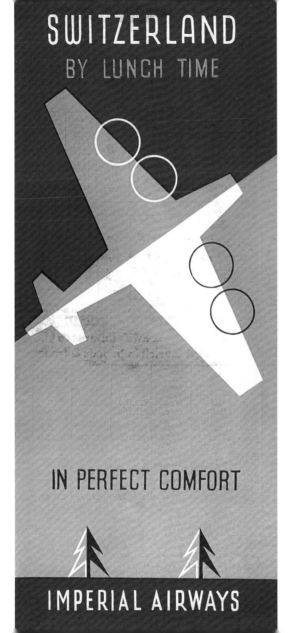

SWITZERLAND
BY LUNCH TIME

IN PERFECT COMFORT

IMPERIAL AIRWAYS

Basle and Zürich, where Imperial Airways takes you so quickly and comfortably are two of the best towns from which to reach the most interesting places in Switzerland. By saving time on the journey you will also have more days to spend on your holidays

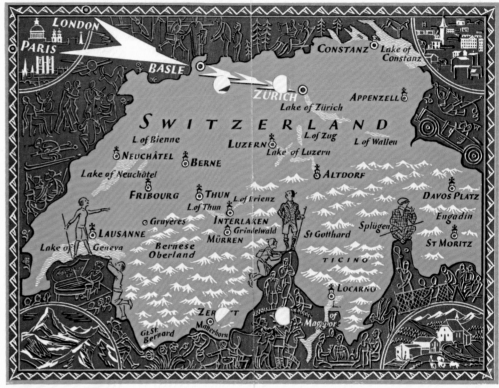

LONDON to **BASLE** in $5\frac{1}{2}$ hours from **£12.15** return

LONDON to **ZÜRICH** in $6\frac{1}{3}$ hrs. from **£13.16** return

BOOK EARLY FOR THE WEEK-END SERVICES

Owing to the great demand for accommodation on the Air Services to Switzerland, we advise you to book as early as possible for the week-end services

Some famous Swiss Peaks

Matterhorn and Dent d'Herens seen from the Mettelhorn

The Bettmeralp near Riederalp, and the Fletschorn and Mischabel Mountains

THE BEAUTY OF SWITZERLAND

No Visit to Europe is complete without seeing Switzerland, its beauty, its gaiety and charm. And BY AIR such a visit is easy and doubly enjoyable

You will have longer in Switzerland if you fly there, and Imperial Airways offers by far the most luxurious passenger air service in the world

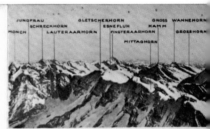

Some famous Swiss Peaks

Lake Cavloccio with Pizzo dei Rossi e Forno-Engadine

(N.B. All these fares are liable to alteration without notice)

IMPERIAL AIRWAYS' FARES TO BASLE AND ZÜRICH IN POUNDS AND FRANCS

Fares must be paid in the currency of the country from which the service is scheduled to leave

A passenger may carry free 15 Kg (33 lbs) of luggage. Every Kg (2.2 lbs) in excess charged. Rate shown below

	LONDON *TO*		*TO* LONDON *FROM*		PARIS *TO*		*TO* PARIS *FROM*		BASLE *TO* ZÜRICH
	BASLE	ZÜRICH	BASLE	ZÜRICH	BASLE	ZÜRICH	BASLE	ZÜRICH	AND ZÜRICH TO BASLE
Single:	£7 0 0	£7 15 0	126 S.Fcs.	141 S.Fcs.	375 F.Fcs.	450 F.Fcs.	70 S.Fcs.	85 S.Fcs.	15 S.Fcs. .. Single
60 Day Return:	£11 18 0	£13 3 6	215 S.Fcs.	240 S.Fcs.	637.50 F.Fcs.	765 F.Fcs.	119 S.Fcs.	144.50 S.Fcs.	25.50 S.Fcs. 60 Day Return
15 Day Return:	£11 4 0	£12 8 0	201 S.Fcs.	225 S.Fcs.	600 F.Fcs.	720 F.Fcs.	112 S.Fcs.	136 S.Fcs.	24 S.Fcs. .. 15 Day Return
Excess Baggage:	1 6	1 8	1.25 S.Fcs.	1.40 S.Fcs.	3.75 F.Fcs.	4.50 F.Fcs.	0.70 S.Fcs.	0.85 S.Fcs.	0.15 S.Fcs. .. Excess Baggage

N-STOP
ONDON TO SWITZERLAND
Y AIR

IME TABLE   Week days only

rvices operated from 20 April to 3 October 1936 inclusive
liable to alteration without notice
24 hour clock is used throughout this timetable

				A	B
LONDON	Airway Terminus		dep	08.25	13.00
LONDON	Air Port	....	dep	09.10	13.45
BASLE	Air Port	....	arr	12.45	16.45
BASLE	Air Port	....	dep	13.00	17.00
ZÜRICH	Air Port	....	arr	13.25	17.25
ZÜRICH	Swissair Offices		arr	14.00	18.00

				B	A
ZÜRICH	Swissair Offices		dep	08.20	14.10
ZÜRICH	Air Port	....	dep	09.00	14.50
BASLE	Air Port	....	arr	09.25	15.15
BASLE	Air Port	....	dep	09.40	15.30
LONDON	Air Port	....	arr	12.50	19.25
LONDON	Airway Terminus		arr	13.35	20.10

vices A operated by Imperial Airways with the *Diana* class of air liner and
vices B by Swissair (using Douglas air liners) for which company Imperial Airways
as the General Agent in Great Britain

mperial Airways & Swissair fares to and
om Basle & Zürich in pounds & francs

		SINGLE	15-DAY RETURN	60-DAY RETURN	*EXCESS BAGGAGE
From LONDON					
to	BASLE	£7.10.0	£12.15.0	£13.10.0	1/6
	ZÜRICH	£8. 2.0	£13,16,0	£14.12.0	1/8
From ZÜRICH					
to	BASLE	15 S.Fs	25.50 S.Fs	27 S.Fs	0.15 S.Fs
	LONDON	132 S.Fs	225.00 S.Fs	238 S.Fs	1.30 S.Fs
From BASLE					
to	LONDON	120 S.Fs	204.00 S.Fs	216 S.Fs	1.20 S.Fs
From BASLE					
to	ZÜRICH	15 S.Fs	25.50 S.Fs	27 S.Fs	0.15 S.Fs

es must be paid in the currency of the country from which the service is
eduled to leave.   N.B.—All fares are liable to alteration without notice
passenger may carry free 15 Kg. (33 lb.) of luggage.   Every Kg. (2.2 lb.) in excess
at rates shown above.   S.Fs Swiss Francs

OOKINGS   FROM

perial Airways Ltd., London : Airway Terminus, Victoria Station, S.W.1.
phone : VICtoria 2211 (Day and Night).—Basle : Swissair Offices, Central
nblatz 3.— Zürich : Swissair, Flugplatz Dübendorf.   Telephone : 934,201.—
w York : The Plaza, Fifth Avenue and 59th Street.   Telephone: Plaza 3-0794
3-1740, or from any office of the Cunard White Star Line in the United
es or travel agents in Europe

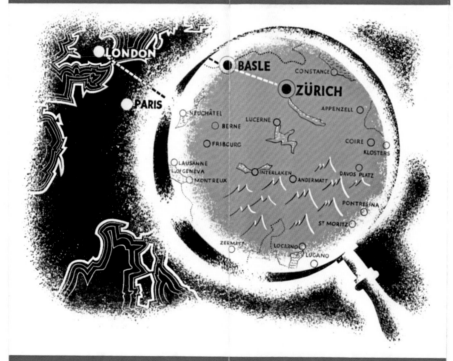

SWITZERLAND BY LUNCH TIME!

From Basle there is an air service by 'Alpar' to Berne and Lausanne which connects with the London Basle service
Twin-engined *Koolhoven* air-liners are used
From Basle, Berne, Zürich and Lausanne there are services to all parts of Switzerland by the Swiss Federal Railways
Full information from the principal Travel Agents and any office of the Railways

LONDON TO
(Times are
terminus to
terminus)

BASLE	IN 4 HOURS 50 MINUTES	FROM £12.15.0 RETURN
BERNE	IN 6 HOURS - - - -	FROM £15. 1.0 RETURN
ZÜRICH	IN 5 HOURS 35 MINUTES	FROM £13.16.0 RETURN
LAUSANNE	IN 6 HOURS 30 MINUTES	FROM £16. 3.0 RETURN

★ BOOK   EARLY   FOR   WEEK-END   SERVICES

Owing to the great demand for accommodation on the air services to Switzerland, we advise you to
book as early as possible for the week-end services

An Imperial Airways liner of the *Diana* class

WITH SPEED AND COMFORT

More and more regular visitors to Switzerland fly there. It's such a very pleasant way of travelling and the speed of it enables you to squeeze every ounce of time out of your holiday

Two great air lines operating in conjunction provide two services daily in each direction. Imperial Airways, using four-engined air liners of the *Diana* class and Swissair using twin-engined *Douglas* air liners

You can leave London first thing in the morning and arrive at Basle or Zürich by lunch-time or you can leave after lunch and arrive for cocktails

The saloons are so quiet and comfortable that you won't get the least bit tired. There's plenty of room for your luggage and a lavatory in every air liner

Douglas air liner over the Alps

Mountaineer by Air Line

You can take wings and look down upon snowy peaks, sheer precipices, and the sources of glaciers, icy regions and breathtaking views that only the eyes of the most hardy mountaineers have seen. On fine days comfortable Swissair Air Liners make flights from Zürich to the Glarnese, Bernese, and Valais Alps, also to Mount Blanc from both Zürich and Geneva. Fares are inexpensive. Full particulars from Imperial Airways and Swissair

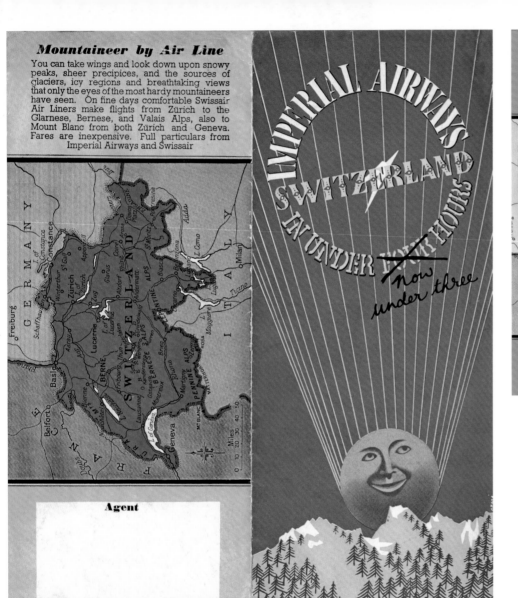

Printed in England by The Whitefriars Press Ltd., London, W.C.1, and published by Imperial Airways Ltd., Airways Terminus, London, S.W. 1A/1547 40M A/39 Stuart

Agent

IMPERIAL AIRWAYS
SWITZERLAND
IN UNDER ~~FOUR~~ HOURS
now under three

Look down on the Alps

Lovely as the Alps are from the ground, the real thrill comes when you see them from the air. On fine days, comfortable Swissair air liners make flights from Zürich to the Glarnese, Bernese and Valais Alps and to Mont Blanc. Also from Geneva to Mont Blanc. These flights introduce you to some of the most glorious views in the world—views that can be had in no other way. Be sure to take your camera. Fares are low. Full particulars from Imperial Airways and Swissair

Agent

Imperial Airways

Switzerland

ee the Alps from a new angle

On fine days, comfortable Swissair air liners make lights from Zürich to the Glarnese, Bernese and Valais Alps and to Mont Blanc. Also from Geneva to Mont Blanc. These flights introduce you to some of the most glorious views in the world—views denied to even the most enthusiastic climbers. Be ure to take your camera. Fares are low. Full information from Imperial Airways or Swissair

AGENT

Printed in Great Britain by the Curwen Press, North Street, E 13
Published by Imperial Airways Ltd., London, England
IA/L/156 45m 5/37 Stuarts

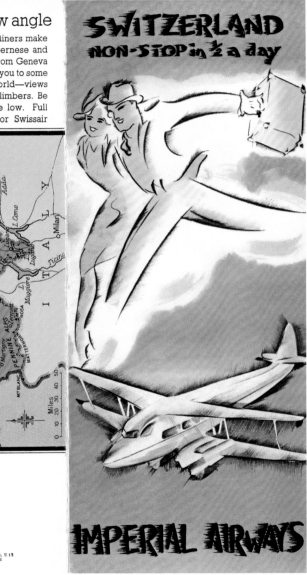

SWITZERLAND
NON-STOP in ½ a day

IMPERIAL AIRWAYS

FLY TO WINTER SPORT

Switzerland in 3 flying hours

IMPERIAL AIRWAYS & SWISSAIR

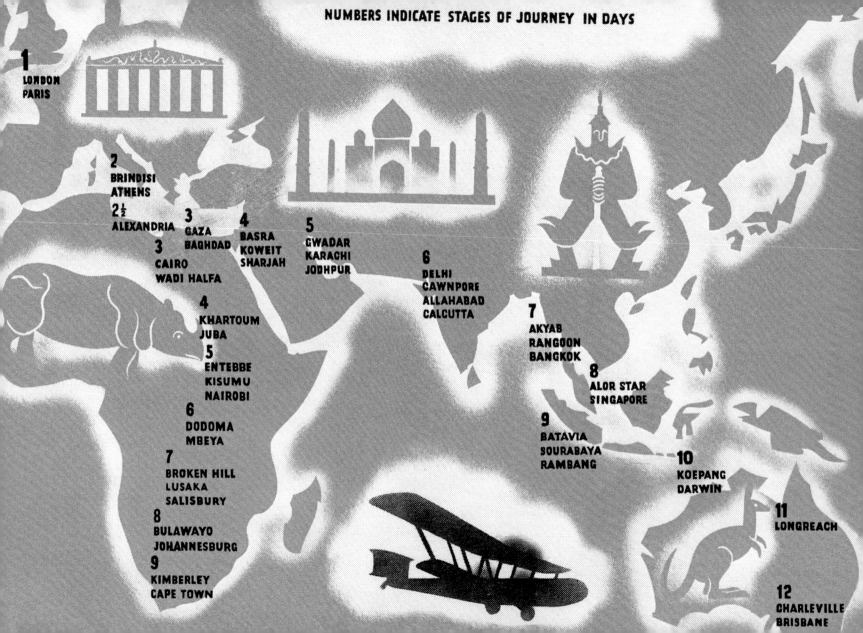

NUMBERS INDICATE STAGES OF JOURNEY IN DAYS

1
LONDON
PARIS

2
BRINDISI
ATHENS
2½
ALEXANDRIA

3
GAZA
BAGHDAD

3
CAIRO
WADI HALFA

4
BASRA
KOWEIT
SHARJAH

4
KHARTOUM
JUBA

5
GWADAR
KARACHI
JODHPUR

5
ENTEBBE
KISUMU
NAIROBI

6
DELHI
CAWNPORE
ALLAHABAD
CALCUTTA

6
DODOMA
MBEYA

7
AKYAB
RANGOON
BANGKOK

7
BROKEN HILL
LUSAKA
SALISBURY

8
ALOR STAR
SINGAPORE

8
BULAWAYO
JOHANNESBURG

9
BATAVIA
SOURABAYA
RAMBANG

9
KIMBERLEY
CAPE TOWN

10
KOEPANG
DARWIN

11
LONGREACH

12
CHARLEVILLE
BRISBANE

This spread, next two spreads: By contrast with its European promotions, Imperial Airways had all the mystery and allure of the far-flung places of the British Empire with which to embellish its long-haul overseas advertising. Using all the skills and imagination of its agency creatives, Imperial produced many stylised and detailed factual and artistic representations of the world routes and places that it served and the aircraft it operated. Imperial also used many quite simple, purely informative geographical maps and diagrammatic illustrations. For Imperial's long-haul services with many stops en route, a diagrammatic map made a lot of sense in clarifying the route to be taken and the places served.

INDIA

BY IMPERIAL
AIRWAYS

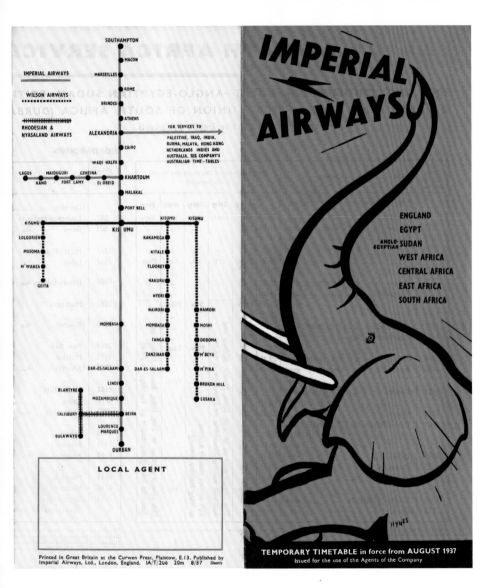

IMPERIAL AIRWAYS

ENGLAND
EGYPT
ANGLO-EGYPTIAN SUDAN
WEST AFRICA
CENTRAL AFRICA
EAST AFRICA
SOUTH AFRICA

TEMPORARY TIMETABLE in force from AUGUST 1937
Issued for the use of the Agents of the Company

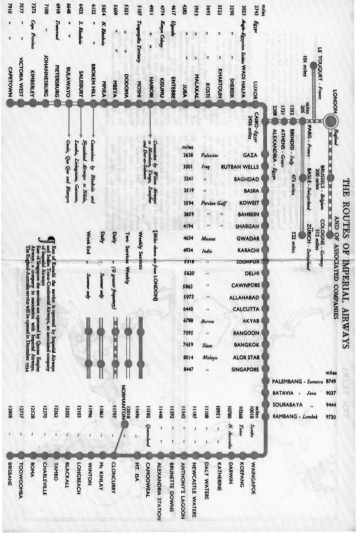

THE ROUTES OF IMPERIAL AIRWAYS AND OF ASSOCIATED COMPANIES

IMPERIAL AIRWAYS MAP OF EMPIRE AIR ROUTES

LONDON TO BRISBANE — 12,754 MILES IN 12½ DAYS

DAILY STAGES LONDON	PARIS	ROME	BRINDISI, ATHENS	GAZA,	BASRA - KOWEIT BAHREIN	GWADAR - KARACHI	DELHI - CAWNPORE ALLAHABAD	AKYAB - RANGOON	ALOR STAR - PENANG	BATAVIA - SOURABAYA	KOEPANG	DALY WATERS NEWCASTLE WATERS DAUNETTE DOWNS CAMOOWEAL MT. ISA WINTON	BLACKALL CHARLEVILLE ROMA, 12,754 Miles TO BRISBANE IN 12½ DAYS
SERVICE TO BRISBANE AS IN OPERATION 1 APRIL, 1935. LIABLE TO ALTERATION WITHOUT NOTICE		2,308 Miles	3,187 Miles	4,140 Miles	5,264 Miles	6,386 Miles		7,405 Miles	8,393 Miles	9,676 Miles	10,726 Miles	12,049 Miles	
ACROSS EUROPE	ACROSS EUROPE	ALEXANDRIA	BAGHDAD	SHARJAH	JODHPUR	CALCUTTA	BANGKOK	SINGAPORE	RAMBANG	DARWIN	LONGREACH		

EXISTING ROUTES
ROUTES IN CONTEMPLATION
IMPORTANT CONNEXIONS OR LIKELY CONNEXIONS

LONDON TO CAPE TOWN — 7,862 MILES IN 9 DAYS

EUROPEAN SERVICES

Imperial Airways operates daily services between London and Paris and every weekday between London, Brussels, Cologne, Leipzig, Prague, Vienna and Budapest. During the summer there are services every weekday between London, Paris, Basle and Zurich, and week-end services to Le Touquet.

Railway Air Services, an associated company of Imperial Airways, operates daily services in the United Kingdom of Great Britain and Northern Ireland

EMPIRE SERVICES

Imperial Airways operates four services weekly between London, Greece and Egypt, two between London and Johannesburg and London and Calcutta and one a week between London and Cape Town and London and Brisbane. There is a service from Nairobi by Wilson Airways to Mombasa (Kenya Colony), Tanga (Tanganyika Territory), Zanzibar

and Dar-es-Salaam (Tanganyika Territory), and by Rhodesia and Nyasaland Airways from Salisbury to Blantyre (Nyasaland), and to Gatooma, Gwe-Gwe, Gwelo and Bulawayo (all Southern Rhodesia) ; there is also a service from Bulawayo to Livingstone, Kalomo, Mazabuka, Lusaka, Broken Hill and Ndola (all Northern Rhodesia). Both Wilson Airways and

Rhodesia and Nyasaland Airways are in association with Imperial Airways. On the India and Australia route the service between Karachi and Singapore is operated by Imperial Airways and Indian Trans-Continental Airways and east of Singapore to Brisbane by Qantas Empire Airways ; both of these companies are in association with Imperial Airways

DAILY STAGES LONDON	PARIS	ROME	BRINDISI, ATHENS	CAIRO, ASSIUT, LUXOR, ASSUAN	KAREIMA, KHARTOUM KOSTI, MALAKAL	ENTEBBE, KISUMU	MOSHI, DODOMA	MPIKA, BROKEN HILL LUSAKA	BULAWAYO, PIETERSBURG	KIMBERLEY, VICTORIA WEST 7,862 Miles TO CAPE TOWN IN 9 DAYS
SERVICE TO CAPE TOWN AS IN OPERATION 1 APRIL, 1935. LIABLE TO ALTERATION WITHOUT NOTICE		2,308 Miles	3,017 Miles	4,216 Miles	4,885 Miles	5,543 Miles	6,374 Miles	7,052 Miles		
ACROSS EUROPE	ACROSS EUROPE	ALEXANDRIA	WADI HALFA	JUBA	NAIROBI	MBEYA	SALISBURY	JOHANNESBURG		

THE EMPIRE ROUTES OF IMPERIAL AIRWAYS

AVION TYPE *ENSIGN* POUR LES SERVICES D'EMPIRE
2 PONTS. 320 Km. HEURE. 20 TONNES

IMPERIAL AIRWAYS

EUROPE • AFRIQUE • INDES • EXTRÊME ORIENT • AUSTRALIE • BERMUDES • NEW YORK

ENGLAND—INDIA—AUSTRALIA SERVICES

ENGLAND — EGYPT — PALESTINE — 'IRAQ — PERSIAN GULF — INDIA — BURMA — SIAM
HONG KONG — MALAYA — AUSTRALIA (Sydney)   •   EASTBOUND SERVICES

Passengers spend the night at:

Southampton, South Western Hotel
Athens, Hotel Grande Bretagne

Basra, Shatt al Arab Hotel (Margil
Airport Hotel)

Karachi, Carlton Hotel
Calcutta, Great Eastern Hotel

Bangkok, Oriental Hotel
Singapore, Raffles Hotel
S.urabaya, Oranje Hotel

Darwin, Resthouse
Townsville, Queen's Hotel

ENGLAND—INDIA—AUSTRALIA
By *Imperial* flying-boat

Miles from South-ampton	Junctions and Termini are shown in CAPITALS	Local Stan-dard Time	Days of Services
			Every
	LONDON (*Waterloo*).......dep.	19 30	Wed., Fri., Sat.
	Southampton *England*.......arr.	21 28	
	SOUTHAMPTON ....dep.	05 15	Thur., Sat., Sun.
624	Marseilles *France*............dep.	10 30	
1005	Rome *Italy*..................dep.	13 35	
1325	Brindisi *Italy*...............dep.	16 15	
1704	Athens *Greece*.............arr.	Even.	
	Athens ....dep.	06 00	Fri., Sun., Mon.
2291	ALEXANDRIA *Egypt* (A).......dep.	14 50	
2644	Tiberias *Palestine**...........dep.	14 50	
3133	Habbaniyeh *'Iraq*‡ ....dep.	19 40	
3446	Basra *'Iraq*...............arr.	Even.	
	Basra ....dep.	05 30	Sat., Mon., Tues.
3791	Bahrein *off Arabia*............dep.	08 35	
4091	Dabai *Oman* ....dep.	11 35	
4831	Karachi *India*...............arr.	Even.	
	Karachi ....dep.	05 00	Sun., Tues., Wed.
5268	Raj Samand *India*...........dep.	08 30	
5538	Gwalior *India* ....dep.	11 00	
5784	Allahabad *India* ....dep.	13 15	
6241	Calcutta *India* ....arr.	Aftn.	
	Calcutta ....dep.	05 30	Mon., Wed., Thur.
6590	Akyab *Burma* ....dep.	09 10	
6911	Rangoon *Burma*.............dep.	12 05	
7282	BANGKOK *Siam* (B).........arr.	Aftn.	
	Bangkok ....dep.	05 30	Tues., Thur., Fri.
7862	Penang *Malaya* ....dep.	11 05	
8253	Singapore *Malaya*...........arr.	Aftn.	
	Singapore ....dep.	08 00	Wed., Fri., Sat.
8816	Batavia *Netherlands Indies*......dep.	13 10	
9278	Sourabaya *Netherlands Indies*...arr.	Aftn.	
	Sourabaya ....dep.	05 30	Thur., Sat., Sun.
10062	Koepang *Netherlands Indies*......dep.	12 50	
10595	Darwin *N. Australia*.......arr.	Even.	
	Darwin ....dep.	06 00	Fri., Sun., Mon.
11382	Karumba *Queensland* ....dep.	13 25	
11798	Townsville *Queensland*........arr.	Aftn.	
	Townsville ....dep.	06 30	Sat., Mon., Tues.
12232	Gladstone *Queensland* ....dep.	10 15	
12506	Brisbane *Queensland* ....dep.	12 55	
12988	SYDNEY *New South Wales*......arr.	Aftn.	

A Junction for East, West and South Africa (see company's Africa timetable)
* For Jerusalem and Tel Aviv
‡ For Baghdad
B Junction for Hong Kong (see timetable overleaf)

ENGLAND—EGYPT
By *Imperial* flying-boat

Miles from South-ampton	Junctions and Termini are shown in CAPITALS	Local Stan-dard Time	Days of Services
			Every
	LONDON (*Waterloo*).......dep.	19 30	Tues., Thur., Fri.
	Southampton *England*.......arr.	21 28	
	SOUTHAMPTON ....dep.	05 45	Wed., Fri., Sat.
624	Marseilles *France*............dep.	11 00	
1005	Rome *Italy*..................dep.	14 05	
1325	Brindisi *Italy* ....dep.	16 45	
1704	Athens *Greece* ....arr.	Even.	
	Athens ....dep.	05 00	Thur., Sat., Sun.
2291	ALEXANDRIA *Egypt*. ....arr.	Morn.	

These services go on to East, West and South Africa

ENGLAND—INDIA By *Imperial* flying-boat to Alexandria, thence by landplane to Calcutta

Miles from South-ampton	Junctions and Termini are shown in CAPITALS	Local Stan-dard Time	Days of Services
			Every
	LONDON (*Waterloo*).......dep.	19 30	Tues., Thur.
	Southampton *England*.......arr.	21 28	
	SOUTHAMPTON ....dep.	05 15	Wed., Fri.
624	Marseilles *France*............dep.	10 30	
1005	Rome *Italy*..................dep.	13 35	
1325	Brindisi *Italy* ....dep.	16 15	
1704	Athens *Greece* ....dep.	Even.	
	Athens ....dep.	06 00	Thur., Sat.
2291	ALEXANDRIA *Egypt* (A).......arr.	Morn.	
	Alexandria ....dep.	13 00	
2599	Lydda *Palestine* ....dep.	17 10	
3163	Baghdad *'Iraq* ....dep.	02 05	Fri., Sun.
3470	Basra *'Iraq* ....dep.	06 25	
3554	Koweit *'Iraq* ....dep.	07 45	
3823	Bahrein *off Arabia*............dep.	11 15	
4147	Sharjah *Oman* ....dep.	15 50	
4884	Karachi *India*................arr.	Morn.	Sat., Mon.
	Karachi ....dep.	04 00	
5271	Jodhpur *India* ....dep.	07 45	
5574	Delhi *India* ....dep.	10 55	
5818	Cawnpore *India*..............dep.	13 05	
5929	Allahabad *India* ....dep.	14 30	
6404	CALCUTTA *India*............arr.	Even.	

🖃 Passengers travel by rail between London and Southampton

Calls will also be made at Macon, Mirabella, Jiwani, Koh Samui, Klabat Bay,
Bima and Groote Eylandt if inducement offers and circumstances permit

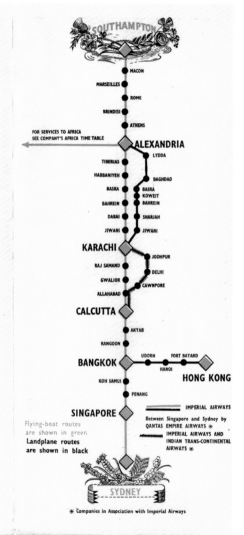

SOUTHAMPTON
MACON
MARSEILLES
ROME
BRINDISI
ATHENS

FOR SERVICES TO AFRICA
SEE COMPANY'S AFRICA TIME TABLE

◆ ALEXANDRIA
LYDDA
TIBERIAS
HABBANIYEH   BAGHDAD
BASRA   BASRA
                KOWEIT
BAHREIN   BAHREIN
DABAI   SHARJAH
JIWANI   JIWANI

KARACHI ◆
RAJ SAMAND   JODHPUR
                     DELHI
GWALIOR   CAWNPORE
ALLAHABAD

CALCUTTA ◆
AKYAB
RANGOON

BANGKOK ◆   UDORN   FORT BAYARD ◆
KOH SAMUI   HANOI   HONG KONG
                   PENANG

SINGAPORE ◆

Flying-boat routes
are shown in green
**Landplane routes
are shown in black**

━━━ IMPERIAL AIRWAYS
Between Singapore and Sydney by
QANTAS EMPIRE AIRWAYS ＊
━━━ IMPERIAL AIRWAYS AND
INDIAN TRANS-CONTINENTAL
AIRWAYS ＊

SYDNEY

＊ Companies in Association with Imperial Airways

This spread, overleaf spread: Imperial Airways promoted both its own services and those of its many partner and associated airlines that linked with its routes, particularly in central and western Africa. Wilson Airways would connect with Imperial at Kisumu using small twin-engine biplanes to fly passengers on to internal destinations that did not warrant a direct service from the UK. In the UK, Railway Air Services would operate to Croydon airport, bringing passengers from the UK provinces to connect on to Imperial's long-haul services. By contrast, Qantas Airways would collect Imperial's passengers at Singapore using the same large flying boats as Imperial, a Short 'C' Class, to fly to Batavia and on to points in Australia. Maps both conventional and diagrammatic were far and away the best method visually to show passengers how these connections worked.

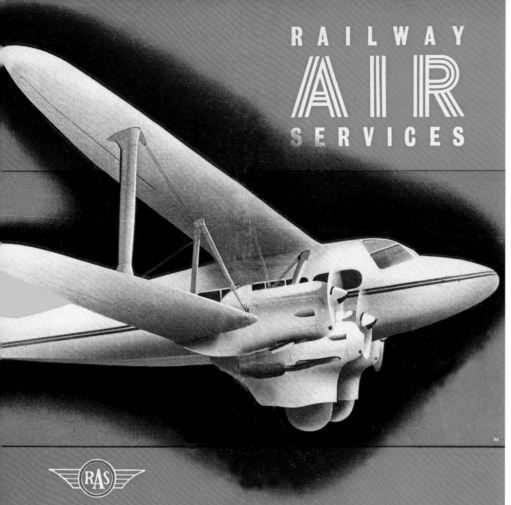

RAILWAY AIR SERVICES

RAS

GENERAL TIME TABLE
INCLUDING SERVICES OF
ISLE OF MAN AIR SERVICES LTD.
JERSEY AIRWAYS LTD.
SCOTTISH AIRWAYS LTD.

GENERAL TIME TABLE
1938

FROM MAY 23rd UNTIL FURTHER NOTICE

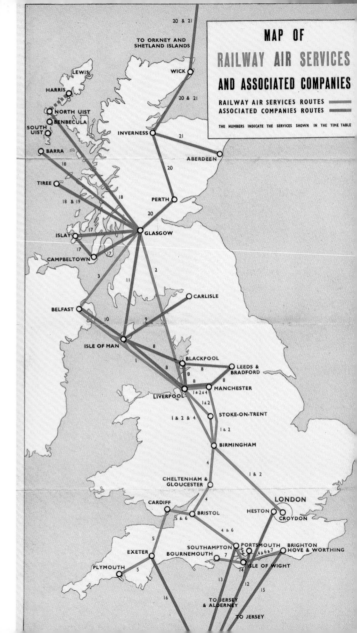

MAP OF
RAILWAY AIR SERVICES
AND ASSOCIATED COMPANIES
RAILWAY AIR SERVICES ROUTES
ASSOCIATED COMPANIES ROUTES
THE NUMBERS INDICATE THE SERVICES SHOWN IN THE TIME TABLE

Qantas Empire Airways

SYDNEY — SINGAPORE
ROUTE MAP

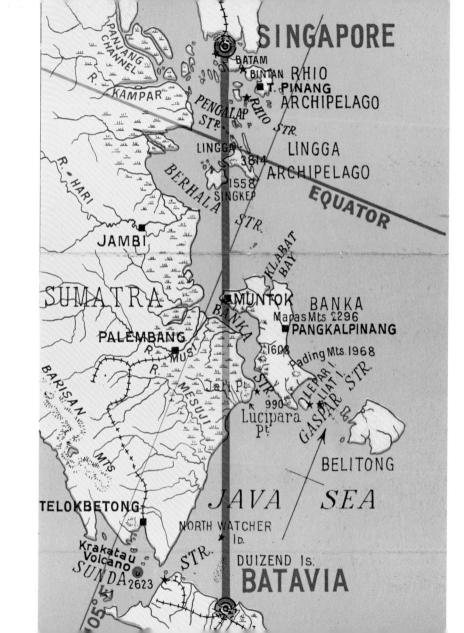

THE EUROPEAN SERVICES OF
BRITISH AIRWAYS

LONDON
HESTON

★ STOCKHOLM
7 HOURS

★ COPENHAGEN
4 HOURS 40 MINUTES

★ HAMBURG
3 HOURS

★ BERLIN
3 HOURS 45 MINUTES

★ WARSAW
6 HOURS 25 MINUTES

★ BRUSSELS
1 HOUR 30 MINUTES

★ FRANKFURT
2 HOURS 30 MINUTES

★ BUDAPEST
6 HOURS 15 MINUTES

★ PARIS
1 HOUR 10 MINUTES

FROM CROYDON
Jointly with Imperial Airways

FOR THE QUICKEST WAY TO HESTON
SEE INSIDE BACK COVER

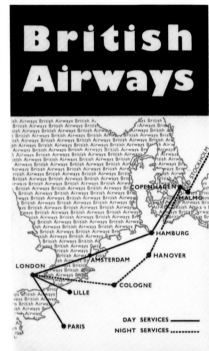

British Airways

DAY SERVICES ————
NIGHT SERVICES ----------

winter timetable
1936-1937

This spread: In 1936 a new airline, British Airways Ltd, was formed from three small, privately owned UK airlines to develop services to northern Europe, the area Imperial Airways was considered to have largely ignored. Being privately owned, British Airways was not restricted on the type of aircraft it could buy, unlike Imperial who were required to buy British to support the UK aircraft manufacturing industry. British Airways chose modern American Lockheed L10s and L14s, twin-engine, all-metal monoplanes, ideal for their relatively short air journeys, and fast, so attractive to businessmen wishing to transact work abroad in a day or two at most. We don't know which advertising agency British Airways used but they did use Theyre Lee-Elliott as an artist, so possibly it was Stuarts Agency. Maps were a common feature in British Airways' advertising, although its simple route structure made them primarily informative rather than artistic. (Opposite middle top and opposite left and right: Theyre Lee-Elliott)

LONDON TO
BERLIN NON-STOP
IN 3¾ HOURS

CENTRAL EUROPE is less than four hours away by British Airways. You sit in an adjustable armchair in the soundproof cabin of an up-to-date airliner, and by the time you've had a meal and a drink you've arrived in Berlin. No changing, no trips, no Customs delays: and valuable days saved for business. British Airways operate their European services every weekday. Ask your travel agent for particulars.

LONDON (Heston) To:

BERLIN in 3¾ hours for £10 10s. | FRANKFURT in 2½ hours for £7 7s.
BRUSSELS in 1¼ hours for £3 15s. | HAMBURG in 3 hours for £6 6s.
COPENHAGEN in 4½ hours for £12 10s. | STOCKHOLM in 7 hours for £17 17s.
| WARSAW in 6½ hours for £14 10s.

AND A LONGER EVERY WEEKDAY. IN PARIS IT ON SUNDAYS
JOINTLY WITH IMPERIAL AIRWAYS FROM CROYDON
YOU CAN SEND YOUR FREIGHT BY ALL THESE CITIES AT ECONOMIC
RATES. TELEPHONE SLOANE 3011.

BRITISH AIRWAYS

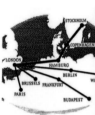

STOCKHOLM IS ONL
7 HOURS AWAY B
BRITISH AIRWAYS

FLYING with British Airways you arrive in Stockholm within of two days. You avoid the nuisance of changing, tip Customs delays, and escape the dirt and fatigue of ordinary travel comfortably in an adjustable armchair. There is a ventilator which regulate yourself. An excellent, freshly-packed lunch is provided. you enjoy some of the most beautiful scenery in Europe.

This service of British Airways to Scandinavia leaves Heston every at 9 a.m. It is part of a network of services in which British Airways the fastest, most comfortable and most modern method of travel in

LONDON (Heston) TO

STOCKHOLM in 7 hours | COPENHAGEN in 4½ ho
FOR £17...0..0 | FOR £12..10..0
BERLIN ..... in 3¾ hours | FRANKFURT .. in 2½ h
FOR £10..0..0 | FOR £7..7..0
BRUSSELS ... in 1¼ hours | HAMBURG ... in 3 h
FOR £3..15..0 | FOR £6..6..0
BUDAPEST ... in 6½ hours | WARSAW .... in 6½ ho
FOR £19..0..0 | FOR £14..10..0

And from Croydon, eight 30-minute services every weekday to Paris 60 f.
Scotland operated jointly with Imperial Airways.
You can send your freight on British Airways routes at economic r
Telephone : Sloane 3011

BRITISH AIRWAY

ENQUIRIES AND TICKETS FROM ALL PRINCIPAL TRAVEL AGENTS
OR BRITISH AIRWAYS LIMITED AT TERMINAL HOUSE, VICTORIA, S.W.1

BRITISH AIRWAYS

SUMMER

TIMETABLE
1939

BELGIUM   DENMARK   ENGLAND   FRANCE
GERMANY   HUNGARY   POLAND   SWEDEN

FROM APRIL 16 UNTIL FURTHER NOTICE

BRITISH AIRWAYS

THE MOST PLEASANT ROUTE TO PARIS
FREQUENT SERVICES DAILY

£6-6-0 WEEK-END RETURN
BOOK YOUR SEAT HERE

B.A. 7   Effective from July 1st, 1936,
until further notice.

B.A. 7   Effective from July 1st, 1936,
until further notice.

BRITISH   BRITISH
AIRWAYS L^{TD}   AIRWAYS L^{TD}

HILLMANS
UNITED
SPARTAN

HILLMANS
UNITED
SPARTAN

BRITISH AIRWAYS

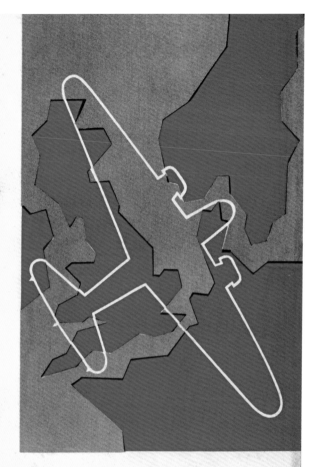

ROUTE MAP

FOR PASSENGERS

HOLIDAYS BY

IMPERIAL AIRWAYS

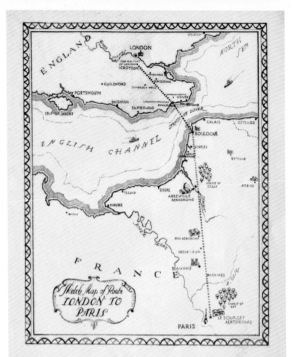

This page: Imperial Airways were also involved in the development of the first inclusive tour holidays in the early 1930s. Considered to be the first such tour was a trip to Paris by the Polytechnic Touring Association, who included a nicely illustrated map of the route in their brochure. In these early days of air travel, the flight itself would have been seen as just as interesting and exciting as the land portion of the tour, so worth illustrating in itself. Another attractive brochure from the mid-1930s advertises European motor tours by Daimlerways. They cooperated with Imperial Airways in offering some of the earliest inclusive tour holidays. Imperial would fly passengers to Paris or Basle where Daimlerways would collect them to commence a 'motor tour' of a quite wide range of destinations in the Dolomites, Switzerland and central Europe.

Opposite and overleaf spread: This rather attractive modernist route map design by Lee-Elliott for Imperial Airways advertises the European cities served and also countries further afield. What appears out of place among this well-known list of names is Le Touquet. This was hardly a European capital but it was an important destination for Imperial's well-heeled customers wishing to take a weekend break on the French coast and sample the delights, or frustrations, of the casinos and local golf courses. The sandy beaches were pretty good too. (Opposite, second overleaf right and left: Theyre Lee-Elliott)

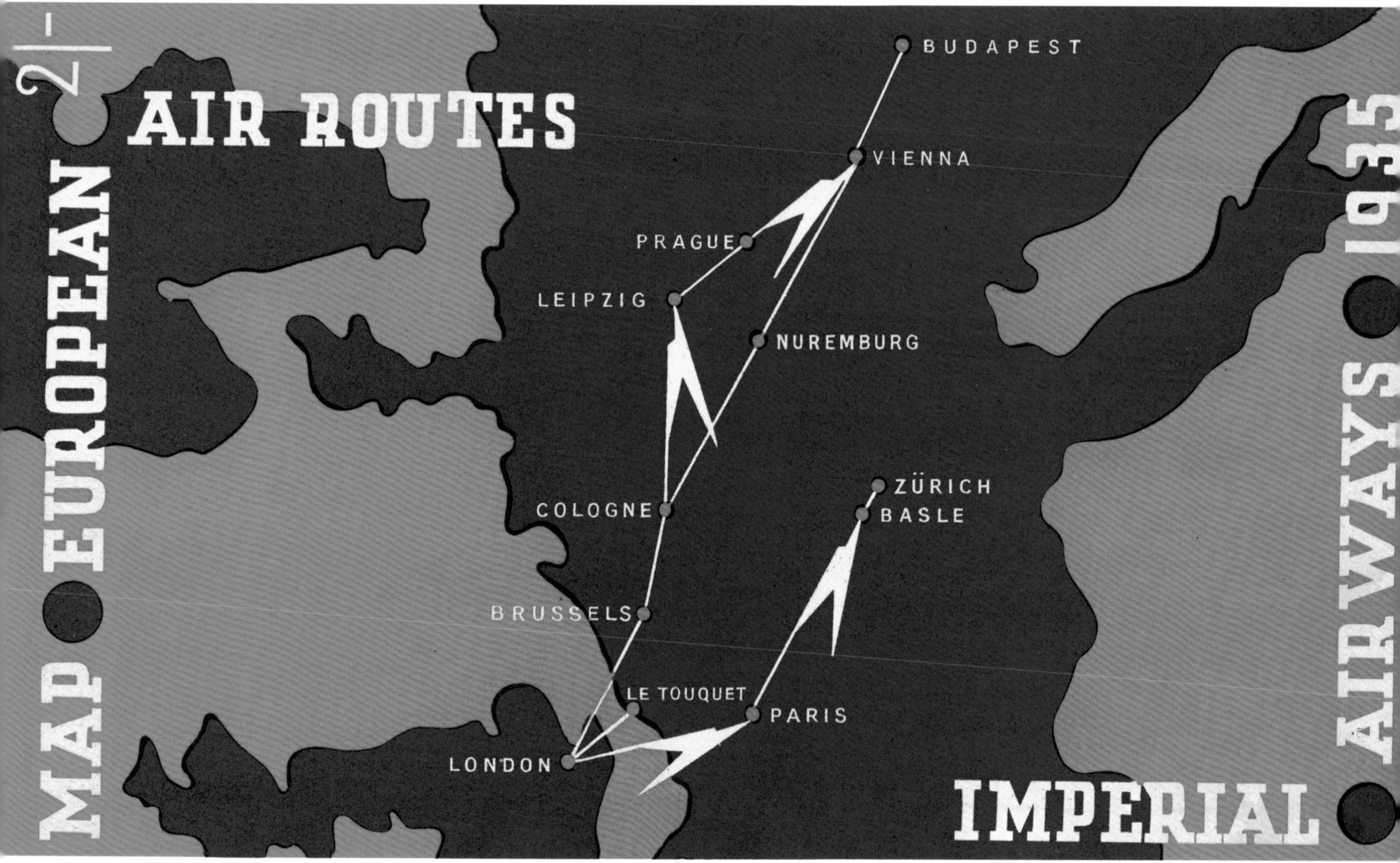

2/-

MAP ● EUROPEAN

AIR ROUTES

AIR WAYS ● 1935

BUDAPEST

VIENNA

PRAGUE

LEIPZIG

NUREMBURG

COLOGNE

ZÜRICH
BASLE

BRUSSELS

LE TOUQUET
PARIS

LONDON

IMPERIAL

6 P.M. IN LONDON

7.45 P.M. IN LE TOUQUET

and this includes tea at the
Casino and dinner in the air

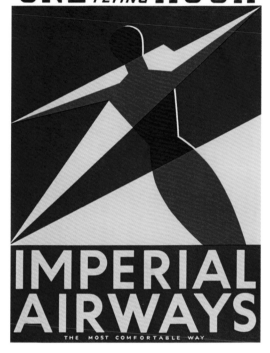

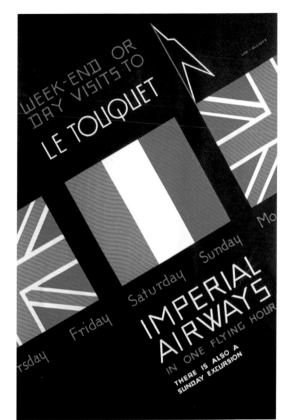

Overleaf: The first airmail service between the UK and Australia was in April 1931 and took twenty days to complete the 13,523-mile journey, two weeks faster than by ship. Airmail rapidly became the preferred choice to send urgent mail abroad, whatever the destination, but it was still expensive and out of the reach of many small businesses and ordinary people; it would also take nearly four more years before Imperial Airways had the resources to start a regular UK–Australia mail service. The breakthrough came in December 1934 with the announcement by the British government that it was to introduce an Empire Air Mail scheme, with all mail carried at one and a half pence for a half-ounce letter between the UK and all British overseas territories. This was a major boost for Imperial Airways who, anticipating a major surge in demand for the service, ordered twenty-eight new high-performance flying boats for its empire services, the Short 'C' Class, as well as seventeen other new aircraft for its European services. (Overleaf left and top: GPO)

MAILS FOR

EAST AND SOUTH AFRICA INDIA MALAYA ETC.

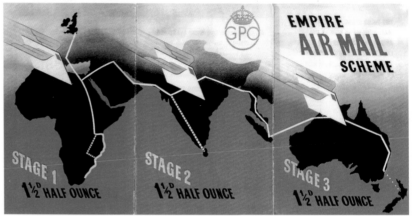

EMPIRE AIR MAIL SCHEME

GPO

STAGE 1
1½ᴰ HALF OUNCE

STAGE 2
1½ᴰ HALF OUNCE

STAGE 3
1½ᴰ HALF OUNCE

THE NEW EMPIRE FLYING-BOAT

IMPERIAL AIRWAYS

EUROPE · AFRICA · INDIA · CHINA · AUSTRALIA

An interesting piece of promotional artistry depicting Imperial Airways' new fleets of land and sea planes, ordered as a result of the introduction of the GPO's Empire Air Mail scheme.

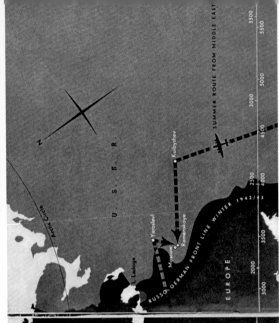

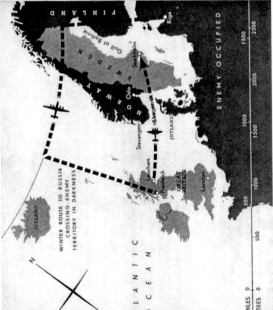

This spread: The six years of conflict during the Second World War effectively shut down commercial civil flying, with all BOAC's aircraft pressed into war service. There is no documentary evidence to hand that shows any form of maps used for anything other than navigation purposes – hardly surprising given passengers were travelling under orders, meaning no on-board frills or nicely illustrated documents for them during a long period of rationing and austerity. BOAC's aircrews performed some major feats of navigation, considering it was all still based on marine charts, radio beacons and celestial sightings combined with dead reckoning. BOAC's exploits in the war years were later recorded by the British Air Ministry in a book called *Merchant Airmen*, now long out of print. It contains a number of maps recording BOAC's support for the war effort and several are included here.

Below and opposite, bottom: The North Atlantic was navigated for the first time ever in both winter and summer during the Second World War, with the winter operations often in total darkness, often through storms and often with the ever present danger of ice clouds. A simple map just cannot do justice to these flights, but an image sums up the less than Club Class experience for the passengers, mainly airmen being flown back to the USA and Canada so they could ferry more aircraft across to Great Britain to support the war effort, a vital service. (HMSO)

Right: Another feat of endurance and remarkable navigation skills comprised the so-called 'Horseshoe Route' service between Great Britain and Australia. This was a service that evolved and changed shape as German and Japanese advances during 1940 and 1941 severed parts of the route. The route's distinctive horseshoe shape was originally flown from Durban to Sydney and, eventually, Perth following the fall of south-east Asia. This was almost a service routing like the days of Imperial Airways using a variety of aircraft from flying boats to landplanes and back to flying boats. BOAC's first Boeing aircraft, the Boeing 314 flying boat, performed the long sector around West Africa to Lagos. Landplanes then flew on to connect with Short 'C' class flying boats routing up from Durban and around eastern Africa past the Red Sea and Arabian Gulf to India and Ceylon (now Sri Lanka). A Qantas Airways Catalina flying boat then flew on deep into the Indian Ocean for over twenty flying hours to Perth; with no navigational aids other than celestial sightings, dead reckoning and a fair bit of luck, they rarely failed to arrive safely. (HMSO)

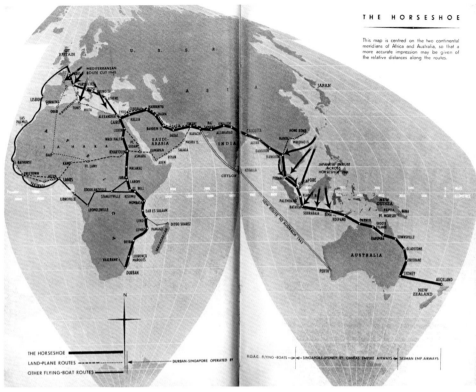

THE HORSESHOE

This map is centred on the two continental meridians of Africa and Australia, so that a more accurate impression may be given of the relative distances along the routes.

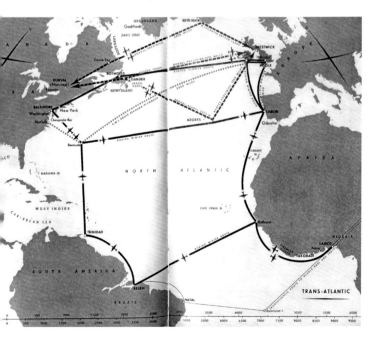

Opposite, far left: The very first flight between Great Britain and Russia took place on 21 October 1942, a journey of some 3,000 miles. The Liberator aircraft took off from Prestwick in Scotland routing due north to the Arctic Circle then due east until the Finnish border and south to Riga before turning east again to Moscow. This was a route never before attempted and timed to fly through darkness over German-held occupied territory. At Ramenskoye airfield, still being used as an operational Russian air force bomber base, Russian and British officials waited. It is documented that with a few minutes to go to the expected arrival time, one of the RAF officers present turned to the Russian officials and advised that the flight could be several hours late due to the difficulty of the routing and winter flying conditions. Almost as he spoke, the sounds of the aircraft's engines could be heard and it landed two minutes later than scheduled, a journey of thirteen hours and nine minutes. That rather sums up the skill and endurance of BOAC's aircrew both in piloting and finding their way through very hazardous skies. (HMSO)

Far left: When civilian flying recommenced in 1946, the British government formed two new nationalised airlines, British European Airways (BEA) and British South American Airways (BSAA), to develop European and Caribbean/South American routes respectively; BOAC would concentrate on the rest of the world. In the early post-war years the three airlines often advertised collectively, primarily to promote travel via their connecting services at London's new airport, Heathrow, but also to reduce their respective advertising budgets. This early poster may well have been commissioned by BOAC as it gives prominence to the North Atlantic route, BEA's and BSAA's global routes being relegated to the globe's margins. It is also believed to be one of the first post-war commissions for Stuarts Agency, being very much in their innovative style. Both BOAC and BEA used Stuarts during the later 1940s. (G. R. Morris)

Left: BOAC set up a design committee in 1946 to look at all aspects of its products and brands with a view to managing their design and presentation standards. One of the committee's consultants was the designer and artist F. H. K. Henrion, and this poster may be by him. The drawing of the aircraft is very much Henrion's style, which together with the transposed photograph and stylised map of BOAC's routes makes for a very attractive and eye-catching advert. The map is central to the advert's message that with BOAC one can 'Speed across the World'.

Next three pages: British South American Airways had a very hard task on their hands to start up from scratch and develop routes to South America and the Caribbean. South America was a very long journey, never flown before commercially and with low prospective passenger numbers. The Caribbean market was more certain except that in the 1940s it had yet to develop into the holiday market that it became in much later decades; in the 1940s it was more about linking Great Britain with its overseas territories and trade than seeking sun. BSAA used maps extensively in their advertising and general promotions as well as on travel documents and route maps for their passengers. Maybe they needed to make sure everyone knew where they flew to and the routes they operated. South America particularly was of little colonial interest to Great Britain, and for many people was nowhere near as familiar as Africa or further east. (Overleaf, bottom right: Gwynn)

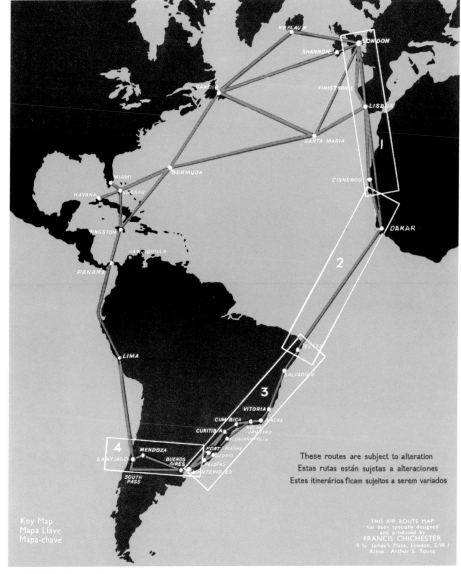

BRITISH SOUTH AMERICAN AIRWAYS

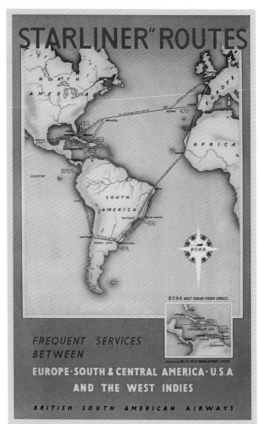

STARLINER" ROUTES

FREQUENT SERVICES
BETWEEN

EUROPE · SOUTH & CENTRAL AMERICA · U.S.A
AND THE WEST INDIES

BRITISH SOUTH AMERICAN AIRWAYS

B.S.A.A. ROUTE → → SOUTH AMERICA TO BRITAIN

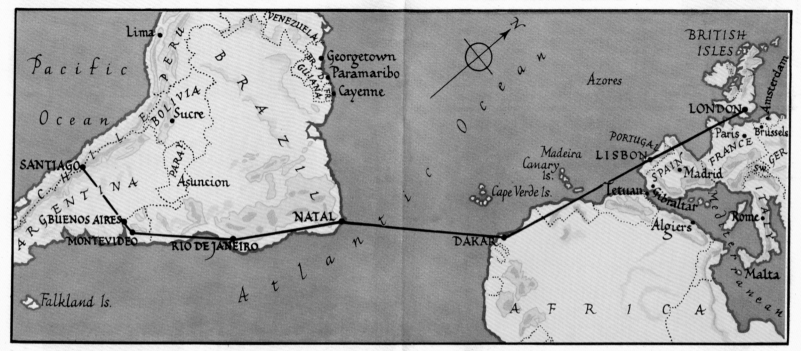

			Kilometres	Statute Miles
SANTIAGO	to LONDON		12599	7836
BUENOS AIRES	to LONDON		11476	7138
MONTEVIDEO	to LONDON		11239	6991
RIO DE JANEIRO	to LONDON		9412	5848
NATAL	to LONDON		7353	4569
DAKAR	to LONDON		4353	2705
LISBON	to LONDON		1566	973

			Nautical Miles	Statute Miles
LONDON	to SANTIAGO		6799	7836
LONDON	to BUENOS AIRES		6193	7138
LISBON	to BUENOS AIRES		5348	6165
DAKAR	to BUENOS AIRES		3844	4433
NATAL	to BUENOS AIRES		2225	2569
RIO DE JANEIRO	to BUENOS AIRES		1114	1290
MONTEVIDEO	to BUENOS AIRES		128	147

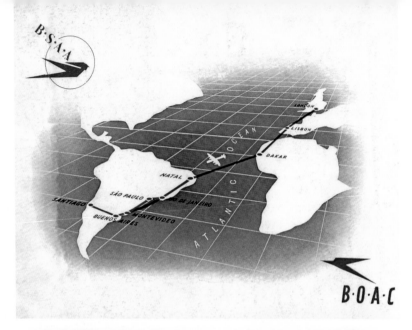

Com Saudações de Natal

de todo o mundo

BRITISH OVERSEAS SOUTH AMERICAN AIRWAYS

Left and below left: BSAA and BOAC advertised together in the later 1940s and maps were the obvious choice to represent their respective routes and links. By then BSAA had extended its routes via the North Atlantic and up the west coast of South America but its business was failing. After the loss of several aircraft in unexplained incidents, it was merged into BOAC in 1949.

Opposite: BOAC also jointly advertised with 'partner' airlines. This was normally with the national airline of the country BOAC was flying to, Qantas Empire Airways (QEA) being a good example and a partner of long standing from the pre-Second World War days of Imperial Airways. To put partnering into its general context, airlines traditionally were only allowed to operate commercially between two separate countries with the approval of both countries' governments, often on a quid pro quo basis, i.e. BOAC would be authorised to fly, say, a weekly service to Australia, provided QEA was authorised to fly to the UK on the same basis. The revenue each earned was often shared (pooled) as well as some costs such as ground handling and joint promotions. In the twenty-first century more flexible operating permissions often now apply, and the application of competition laws, such as in the USA and the European Union, limit or negate commercial airline cooperation. BOAC and QEA's 'Kangaroo Service' was introduced to maximise the rapid opening up of the UK–Australia route after the end of the Second World War. Cooperation and sharing was very important, especially for Great Britain, with its resources (not least in commercial aircraft) being in short supply; one of the maps in the poster adverts rather highlights the latter point, but in QEA's favour. BOAC operated flying boats, Short Hythes and Solents, while QEA operated the most modern commercial aircraft then available, the Lockheed Constellation. The Constellation was not only much more luxurious but could operate longer sectors with fewer stops so a preferred choice for many passengers. Without the partnering arrangement, BOAC would have been very uncompetitive.

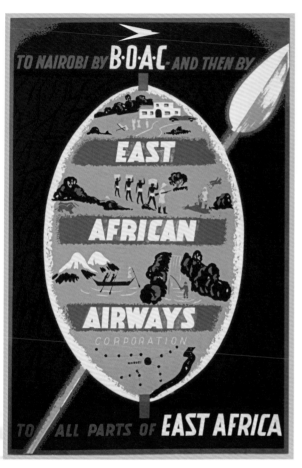

This spread: In 1946 BOAC had acquired the Lockheed Constellation and used it on the North Atlantic routes to New York and Montreal in order to be competitive with the airlines of the USA operating the same aircraft. By the late 1940s BOAC had acquired the new Boeing Stratocruiser to operate on the North Atlantic (and was shortly to retire its flying boats) so switched its Constellations to its eastern routes to augment its older and slower Canadair Argonaut aircraft. Even though this map does not extend to Australia (it is from a brochure promoting travel between 'Britain and Pakistan, India and Ceylon') it refers to BOAC 'in association with QEA' and they would connect with BOAC's services at Colombo. These brochures were a continuation of the style developed by Imperial Airways before the Second World War, with an attractive and glossy front cover, a stylised and similarly attractive route map and photographs and commentary on the points of origin and destination and points en route.

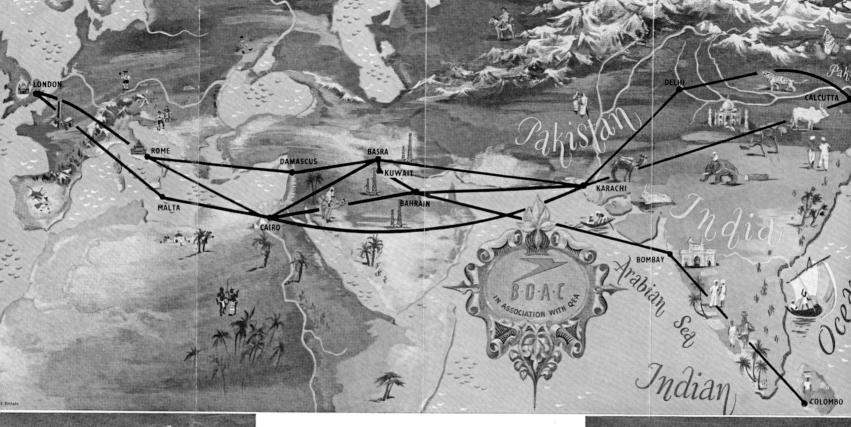

LONDON
ROME
MALTA
DAMASCUS
BASRA
KUWAIT
CAIRO
BAHRAIN
KARACHI
DELHI
CALCUTTA
Pakistan
Pak
India
BOMBAY
Arabian Sea
Ocean
Indian
COLOMBO

B·O·A·C
IN ASSOCIATION WITH QEA

CONSTELLATION SPEEDBIRD (on the left). One of the world's most tried and proved airliners for long range non-stop flights. It can cruise at a speed of 317 m.p.h. and accommodates thirty-eight passengers in deep seated comfort. The aircraft is pressurized.

ARGONAUT SPEEDBIRD (on the right) built for B.O.A.C. by Canadair Ltd. accommodates forty passengers and cruises quietly and majestically at 298 m.p.h. on four Rolls-Royce Merlin engines. Passengers enjoy a new freedom of movement in either of two cabins and in the luxury of the rear lounge which seats six. Pressurized, of course, for over-the-weather flying

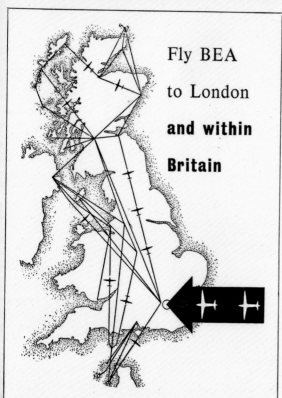

Fly BEA
to London
and within
Britain

Fly BEA from Copenhagen to London. Use the BEA network within Great Britain too—there are regular BEA services between London and Scotland, Belfast, the Isle of Man, the Channel Islands

For courtesy, comfort, speed—always fly BEA

BEA

British European Airways

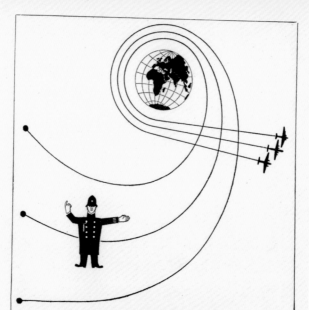

Oslo ➡ *London* ➡ *all parts of the world by British Airways*

Today, and every other day, British airliners are coming in, over the white roofs of eastern cities, over South American jungle, over London haze—on routes all over the world. Britain's three great airlines are the culmination of many years of pioneering and development. They are backed by maintenance and engineering of the highest possible standard. They are flown by the cream of Britain's airmen. And they offer you a traditional courtesy and comfort.

 BOAC   BEA   ➤ BSAA

BRITISH OVERSEAS EUROPEAN S.AMERICAN **AIRWAYS**

SOLPLASSEN I, OSLO. TEL: 42.36.96 & 42.37.02

BRITISH EUROPEAN AIRWAYS
the key to faster travel

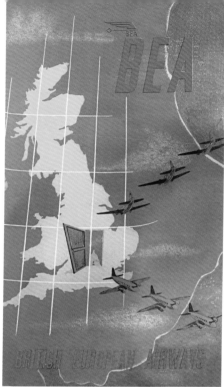

Opposite: With BSAA merged into BOAC in 1949, BOAC and BEA jointly advertised for a few more years. A map was a very clear medium to promote their connecting services, with the artist Henrion depicting a square globe as an interesting and certainly different way to do so. The globe shows the routes in a linear style without place names and is more about emphasising the global spread of the two airlines' services rather than specific countries. BEA often used a linear or diagrammatic style of map in its advertising for many years whereas BOAC tended to use a truer but often stylised map presentation. These very early BEA poster and media adverts from the mid- to late 1940s are very much forerunners of the style. (Opposite bottom right: F.H.K. Henrion; opposite top right: Zero)

Above left and middle: BEA's sometimes quite simple early advertising goes a stage further in this stylised map of Great Britain and the edge of the western European mainland. What is quite different is that there are no city names or routes shown but just an open door in the depiction of the British mainland and a hint of lines of latitude and longitude. BEA's Vickers Viking aircraft are drawn in line astern leaving and arriving through the door. This may be a subtle way of emphasising BEA's extensive network or, possibly, may be a forerunner of a later advertising strapline: 'BEA takes you there and brings you back.'

Above right: Another simple early advert of BEA's that this time very clearly names the cities of London and Brussels, together with an outline of a BEA building, its corporate flag and a silhouette of a Viking aircraft. There's no doubt that it's BEA and no doubting where it's headed, and in a pleasing contemporary style that would soon give way to much more detailed artworks and maps.

Above left: Another contemporary diagrammatic map poster from BEA, but this time advertising one of their 'triangular' UK domestic services from London to Glasgow then Belfast and back to London by a Vickers Viking aircraft.

Above middle and right: Just to explain what a Vickers Viking looks like, BEA often issued quite detailed cutaway promotional material of its aircraft types to show the interior layout and emphasise their 'luxury travel'. It was certainly not luxury by modern standards, but in the context of the time a huge advance in just ten years since the latter days of Imperial Airways.

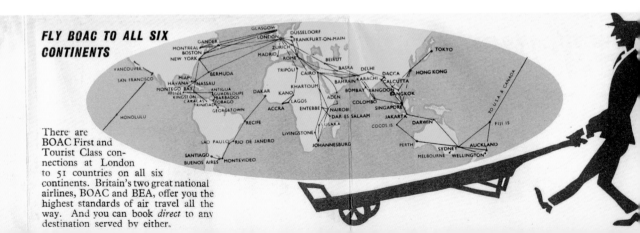

IN EUROPE

MORE PEOPLE FLY BEA

THAN ANY OTHER

AIRLINE

FLY BOAC TO ALL SIX CONTINENTS

There are BOAC First and Tourist Class connections at London to 51 countries on all six continents. Britain's two great national airlines, BOAC and BEA, offer you the highest standards of air travel all the way. And you can book *direct* to any destination served by either.

Opposite bottom, this page and overleaf: By the early 1950s not only had BEA acquired the latest civilian airliners, the Vickers Viscount and the Airspeed Ambassador (Elizabethan), but also a newer, more flamboyant style in its advertising and promotional material. Its route network was expanding fast, with even the eastern Mediterranean and North Africa on offer, so more opportunities for their creative agencies to produce some interesting material in which maps played a strong role. There's even a small plug for BOAC: 'Fly BOAC to all six continents.' (Overleaf left: Ian Ribbons; opposite bottom and this page: P. Temple)

BRITISH EUROPEAN AIRWAYS

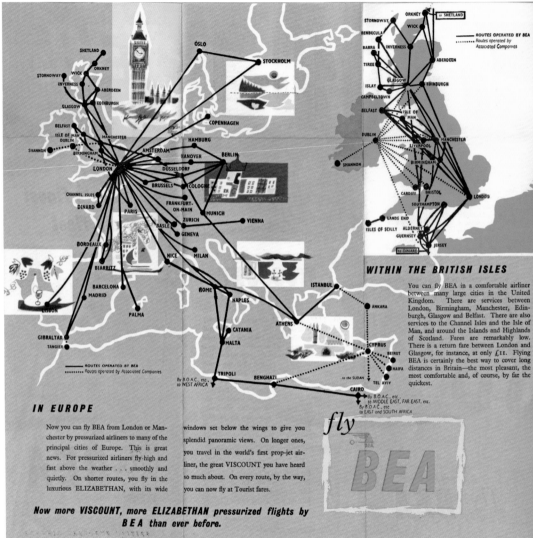

ROUTES OPERATED BY BEA
Routes operated by Associated Companies

WITHIN THE BRITISH ISLES

You can fly BEA in a comfortable airliner between many large cities in the United Kingdom. There are services between London, Birmingham, Manchester, Edinburgh, Glasgow and Belfast. There are also services to the Channel Isles and the Isle of Man, and around the Islands and Highlands of Scotland. Fares are remarkably low. There is a return fare between London and Glasgow, for instance, at only £11. Flying BEA is certainly the best way to cover long distances in Britain—the most pleasant, the most comfortable and, of course, by far the quickest.

ROUTES OPERATED BY BEA
Routes operated by Associated Companies

IN EUROPE

Now you can fly BEA from London or Manchester by pressurized airliners to many of the principal cities of Europe. This is great news. For pressurized airliners fly high and fast above the weather . . . smoothly and quietly. On shorter routes, you fly in the luxurious ELIZABETHAN, with its wide windows set below the wings to give you splendid panoramic views. On longer ones, you travel in the world's first prop-jet airliner, the great VISCOUNT you have heard so much about. On every route, by the way, you can now fly at Tourist fares.

fly
BEA

Now more VISCOUNT, more ELIZABETHAN pressurized flights by BEA than ever before.

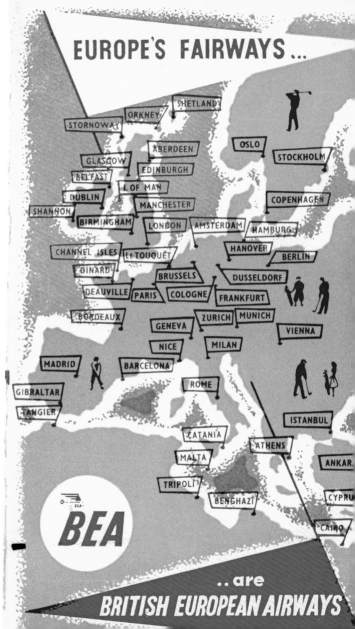

This page and overleaf: This map does not quite indicate a BEA wish to take on the world as it is primarily about promoting its European flights connecting with other airlines to other continents. However, BEA were keen to fly directly to more points in the Middle East other than Tel Aviv and had quickly grabbed Beirut when BOAC pulled out, much to BOAC's annoyance. This ambition did much to sour relations with BOAC, who considered the Middle East their sphere of influence, and joint promotions appear to fall rapidly away in later years. This map brochure also continues the tradition of providing some information on places of interest on BEA's routes, pretty equally split between business and holiday destinations. The Mediterranean sunspots were important revenue earners for BEA and they heavily promoted holiday business and specialist tours such as golfing holidays.

More than 75 places to visit on the **BEA** network

AND HUNDREDS MORE BY CONVENIENT CONNECTING RAIL AND ROAD SERVICES

LONDON *Convenient onward flights to key cities in Britain; including Manchester, Belfast, Edinburgh, Glasgow—with connexions for the Islands and Highlands of Scotland.*

ROME *The 'Eternal City' is an important point on the BEA network, having connexions to the Riviera, Eastern Mediterranean, Malta and North Africa.*

NICE *On one of the main BEA routes to London from Rome and North Africa. Nice has road connexions for the whole Riviera— including Juan-les-Pins, Cannes, Monte Carlo and Menton.*

MILAN *Another important BEA destination on one of the main north-south routes, Milan is only one hour from Lake Como; and well situated for visiting Bergamo, Mantua and Cremona.*

ATHENS *Another of the world's great ancient and modern cities. Fast BEA connexions to Rome, Milan, Munich, London, Istanbul and many points in the Levant.*

MADRID *Centre of Spain and all that is Spanish; excursions can be made from Madrid to Avila, Segovia, Toledo, El Escorial and Alcala de Henares.*

Just a few of the main business and holiday centres on BEA's great European network—which links over 75 principal cities

TANGIER *Colourful city of Morocco. Convenient sea/air connexions over the straits to Gibraltar. For Southern Spain; and for direct BEA services to London.*

MUNICH *A wonderful tourist centre for the valleys, hills and lakes of the Bavarian Alps. Direct BEA connexions for Athens and London.*

OSLO *For business and pleasure in Norway, Oslo is your best centre. Fast, direct BEA flights to London; and on to Stockholm for Helsinki.*

ZURICH *For business, for summer holidays, for winter sports. Fast and frequent BEA flights to and from London; direct onward BEA flights to Belgrade.*

DUSSELDORF *One of the great European business centres on the BEA network; fast, regular flights to and from London; and direct onward flights to Berlin.*

NAPLES *For the lovely Bay of Naples, Capri, Ischia, Sorrento, and Amalfi. Direct BEA flights to London; and south by BEA to Malta and Tripoli.*

Right: BEA was also a leader in promoting new fare types to try and attract more passengers. Cheap night flights were one way to fill up aircraft in the off-peak period and keep the aircraft flying. Aircraft are notoriously expensive when sitting on the ground, not earning their keep while still incurring costs such as expensive airport parking charges.

Your Route Map and Your Flight

BEA is proud to serve you as your national British airline charged with responsibility for air routes in the United Kingdom and the European and Mediterranean areas. As a scheduled airline, our first objectives are to run safely, regularly and punctually and to give you the service you require. We want to make flying with BEA a pleasant, matter-of-fact, everyday affair offering you that personal attention which we regard as an important part of our job. Naturally, we would like our passengers to make a habit of it, but that is not to say that we want to take the romance out of "flying BEA." The fascination of watching countries unfold below as we ride on our way at twenty thousand feet or so surely never palls, and there is always that pleasurable thrill when some landmark on our route map is identified, especially one personally well known. Many of our passengers tell us that this adds to the enjoyment of the flight, and we have been encouraged by this to improve our route maps from year to year. This is the latest edition.

An interesting point you will see from these maps is that we do not always fly on a direct course. Only a few years ago a straight line from airport to airport could be taken. But, as air traffic has grown so have the regulations to ensure the safety of the flow of aircraft from city to city. Clearly defined "Airways" have been established between major airports. These Airways are like aerial

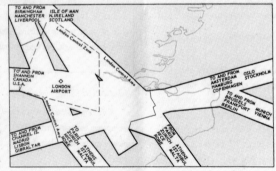

DIAGRAM OF AIRWAYS AND CONTROL POINTS INTO LONDON

highways along which air traffic is much more carefully regulated than in earthbound traffic on the finest roads. Along the Airways, automatic radio beacons send up the reassuring call unhampered by bad weather. As each beacon is passed the exact position of the aeroplane in the air is reported to the Air Traffic Control Centres, where it is plotted with the positions of all other aircraft using the Airway so that their courses can with certainty be kept safely apart. The diversion from a straight course from airport to airport is part of this carefully planned machinery for ensuring the orderly and safe progress of aircraft into and out of great cities.

Throughout your flight, radio checks will be made on the weather on the route, at the destination and at other carefully selected airports in case the weather at your destination is too bad for landing. Nowadays, of course, these occasions are rare, because BEA aircraft are equipped with radio and radar devices which enable your Captain to descend through dense cloud with absolute confidence and certainty.

But, even with these aids, he will never try to land unless he is sure that he can do so with safety. He has been flying for many years as a First Officer even before he was given command, and his immense experience — probably more than a million miles of flying—is backed up by continual refresher training and

Left, opposite and overleaf: It is unclear whether BEA or BOAC led the way in a return to the printed flight guides (map books) for passengers introduced by Imperial Airways, but now with a more 1950s modern twist on their cover designs. These BEA editions from the early 1950s were almost like atlases in their presentation and style, with three-dimensional relief maps making it very easy, on a clear day, to map-read oneself across the UK or Europe. Some guides even included a diagram of the main airways to and from London Airport (Heathrow), the reason being to allay passengers' air safety fears, carefully explaining that the routes flown were not always in a straight line due to the density of air traffic, but that it was all carefully coordinated by air traffic control; while it all looked complex and very busy, aircraft moved in an 'orderly and safe progress' (something travellers today, if they think about it at all, take for granted). These detailed guides were given away for free to every passenger (Imperial Airways used to sell theirs), quite a cost given BEA were reported as carrying more passengers in Europe than any other airline.

BEA
ROUTE MAP
For the UNITED KINGDOM
Channel Islands & Isle of Man

CONTINENTAL ROUTE MAPS

BEA

BEA

CONTINENTAL ROUTE MAPS

BRITISH EUROPEAN AIRWAYS · BRITISH EUROPEAN AIRWAYS

BEA
continental
route maps

BEA takes you there   and BEA brings you back

BEA

BEA

INTERNATIONAL
ROUTE MAPS

INTERNATIONAL
ROUTE MAPS

BRITISH EUROPEAN AIRWAYS   BRITISH EUROPEAN AIRWAYS

Opposite: This is a very early 1946 poster from BOAC in a series issued before it had commenced its first North Atlantic commercial service to New York on 1 July 1946 – the route is just pencilled in. The strapline, 'Speedbird routes – across the world', was neatly emphasised by an outline of most of the world; the Americas would come later.

Above: The 'routes across the world' theme continues, this time enhanced by the message that there are 5,000 BOAC travel agents throughout the world. The secondary message is that agents open the door to world travel on BOAC. It also unintentionally made clear that BOAC, and most other airlines, were for many decades highly reliant on independent travel agents selling their services. Without travel agents, no airline would have the financial means and resources to have their own offices worldwide except in the main cities to which they flew. That situation rapidly began to change in the later 1990s as the development of the internet and airline reservation systems enabled airlines to sell directly into customers' homes and offices.

SPEEDBIRD ROUTES...ACROSS THE WORLD

B·O·A·C

BRITISH OVERSEAS AIRWAYS CORPORATION IN CONJUNCTION WITH QANTAS EMPIRE AIRWAYS, SOUTH AFRICAN AIRWAYS AND TASMAN EMPIRE AIRWAYS

BOAC's advertising continued using artistic licence in depicting its worldwide spread in a variety of posters that evolved its earlier strapline into 'It's a small world by Speedbird', and even 'It's a smaller world by Speedbird'. BOAC's Speedbird symbol is a central feature of each poster, with Henrion's abstract take on it presenting the face of the globe, a striking and memorable feature, thus doing its job well as a promotional medium. Pick's is equally interesting, although her take on the globe is more sixteenth than twentieth century. (Left: F. H. K. Henrion; right: Beverley Pick)

This page, next six pages: Throughout the 1950s BOAC also continued to use maps widely in their advertising and promotional material; these were often simple Mercator's projections but occasionally used something much more interesting such as an Oblique Mercator. Brochures for use in BOAC's travel agency offices were used extensively both to sell tickets and for use when travelling. The centrefolds were often a traditional and lightly stylised world map, often headed by the caption 'The World Wide Airline', which BOAC really was in that it flew to all six continents. It did not technically span the globe – until the later 1950s, BOAC did not fly itself across the Pacific except using by using a partner airline. The maps are a fascinating evolution of BOAC's route network, the black route line markings becoming denser as the years progress and new routes are introduced. The brochures also represent an attractive collection of artworks, both on their covers and inside, depicting sights and events of interest to passengers such as Her Majesty the Queen's Coronation in 1953. (Above right: Adelman; third page, right: Negus/Sharland; fourth page: Reitz; fifth page, left: Adelman; fifth page, bottom right: Reitz; sixth page: Adelman)

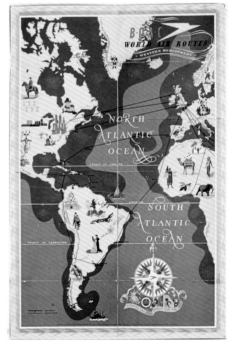

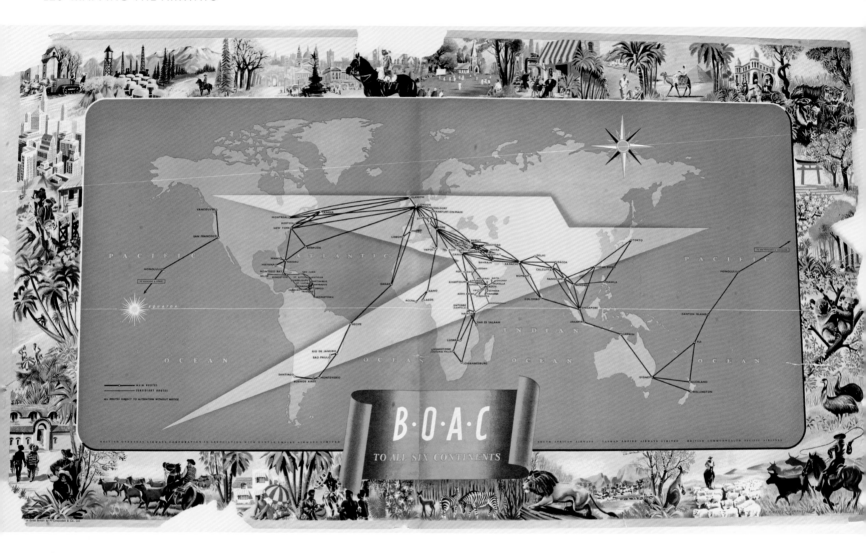

NORTH AMERICA · EUROPE · ASIA · PACIFIC OCEAN · ATLANTIC · SOUTH AMERICA · OCEAN · AFRICA · INDIAN OCEAN · AUSTRALIA

B·O·A·C SPEEDBIRD ROUTES LINKING ALL SIX CONTINENTS

BRITISH OVERSEAS AIRWAYS CORPORATION IN ASSOCIATION WITH QANTAS EMPIRE AIRWAYS LIMITED · SOUTH AFRICAN AIRWAYS AND TASMAN EMPIRE AIRWAYS

B·O·A·C FLIES TO ALL SIX CONTINENTS

B.O.A.C. operates world-wide in association with ADEN AIRWAYS LTD · AIR-INDIA INTERNATIONAL · BAHAMAS AIRWAYS LTD · BRITISH WEST INDIAN AIRWAYS · CATHAY PACIFIC AIRWAYS
CENTRAL AFRICAN AIRWAYS CORPORATION · EAST AFRICAN AIRWAYS CORPORATION · GHANA AIRWAYS · GULF AVIATION · KUWAIT AIRWAYS
MALAYAN AIRWAYS · MIDDLE EAST AIRLINES · NIGERIA AIRWAYS · QANTAS EMPIRE AIRWAYS LTD · SOUTH AFRICAN AIRWAYS
TASMAN EMPIRE AIRWAYS LTD · TRANS-CANADA AIRLINES

fly by B·O·A·C

AROUND THE WORLD

BRITISH OVERSEAS AIRWAYS CORPORATION

THE WORLD WIDE AIRLINE

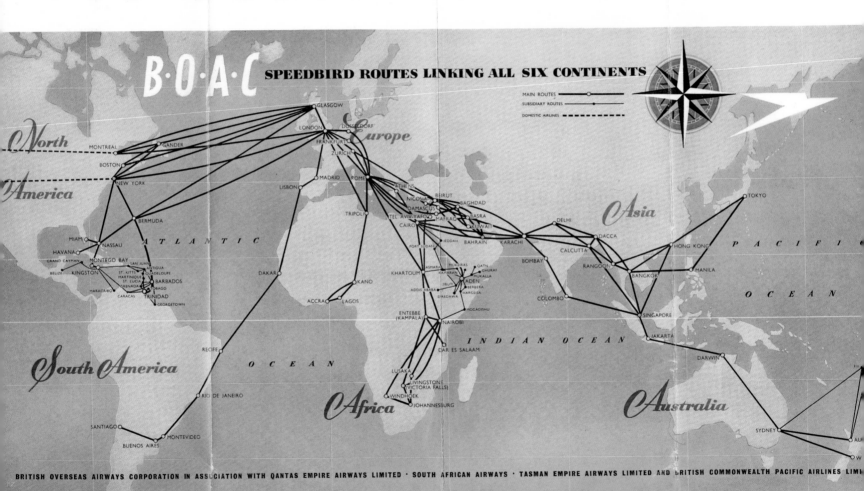

B·O·A·C SPEEDBIRD ROUTES LINKING ALL SIX CONTINENTS

MAIN ROUTES
SUBSIDIARY ROUTES
DOMESTIC AIRLINES

North America · *South America* · *Europe* · *Asia* · *Africa* · *Australia*

BRITISH OVERSEAS AIRWAYS CORPORATION IN ASSOCIATION WITH QANTAS EMPIRE AIRWAYS LIMITED · SOUTH AFRICAN AIRWAYS · TASMAN EMPIRE AIRWAYS LIMITED AND BRITISH COMMONWEALTH PACIFIC AIRLINES LIMITED

FLY BY B·O·A·C
AROUND THE WORLD

BRITISH OVERSEAS AIRWAYS CORPORATION

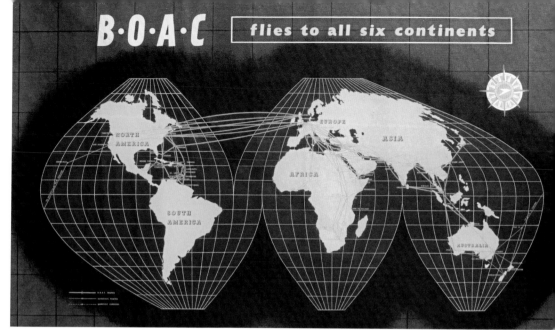

B·O·A·C flies to all six continents

NORTH AMERICA

EUROPE

ASIA

AFRICA

SOUTH AMERICA

AUSTRALIA

B·O·A·C the world wide Airline

This map is drawn on an Oblique Mercator Projection, which enables important but unfamiliar aspects of the world to be represented. This Projection overcomes the disadvantages of a Globe, on which it is impossible to see more than part of one hemisphere at a time, and a normal Mercator Projection, which shows neither the polar regions themselves nor the relation of the continents across the polar regions.

Opposite and overleaf: BOAC's map route guides, like BEA's, began to resemble real atlases with attractively designed covers and easy-to interpret three-dimensional maps. They had evolved since the late 1940s/early 1950s versions, which involved a copy of the aircraft's flight navigation chart being handed around to passengers annotated by the crew with details of the flight's progress. These were soon turned into proper guides, with the early versions even including a convenient globe to put the relevant map section into a global context. In later years the guides were expanded to contain detailed flight information and became quite weighty, but still free, passenger giveaways. From the 1950s to 1970s most international airlines were heavily restricted by international agreements on what they could give away to their economy passengers, so an attractive map guide with useful information all went towards trying to gain a competitive edge. (Opposite right and overleaf left: Laban)

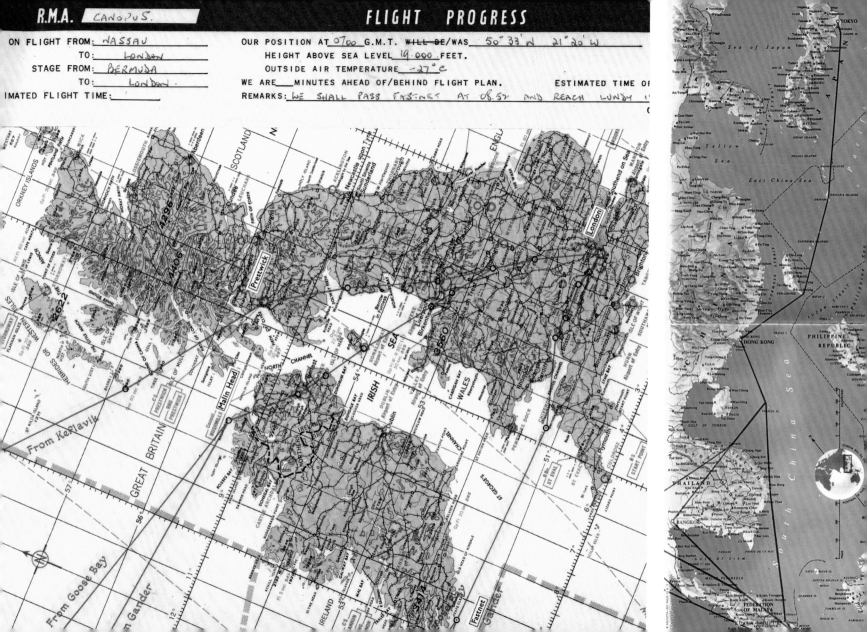

R.M.A. CANOPUS.
FLIGHT PROGRESS

ON FLIGHT FROM: NASSAU

TO: LONDON

STAGE FROM: BERMUDA

TO: LONDON.

IMATED FLIGHT TIME: _____

OUR POSITION AT 0700 G.M.T. WILL BE/WAS 50° 33' N 21° 20' W

HEIGHT ABOVE SEA LEVEL 19.000 FEET.

OUTSIDE AIR TEMPERATURE -27° C

WE ARE _____ MINUTES AHEAD OF/BEHIND FLIGHT PLAN.   ESTIMATED TIME OF

REMARKS: WE SHALL PASS FASTNET AT 08.52 AND REACH LUNDY

B·O·A·C ROUTE MAP No. 2

BRITAIN · MIDDLE EAST · AUSTRALIA · FAR EAST

B·O·A·C ROUTE MAP * FLIGHT INFORMATION

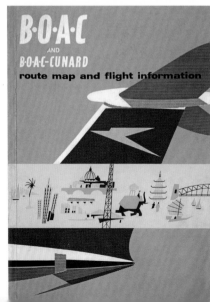

B·O·A·C AND B·O·A·C-CUNARD route map and flight information

BEA Comet 4B

BUILT BY DE HAVILLAND

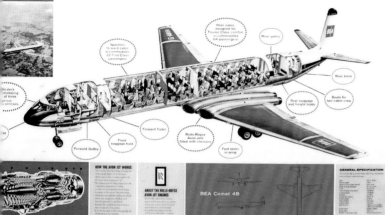

POWERED BY 4 ROLLS-ROYCE AVON TURBO-JETS

Comet 4B speeds your journey

WHAT YOU WILL WANT TO KNOW ABOUT THE Comet 4B

BOAC and BEA were understandably keen to promote the introduction of new aircraft types into their fleets. As the 1950s closed and commercial jet aircraft began to become widely available on both long-haul (intercontinental) and short-haul (European) routes, their higher speeds and shorter journey times made them the must-have equipment and mode of travel for airlines and passengers alike. The Boeing 707 and Comet 4 were BOAC's two long-haul jets, with the 707 used initially on North Atlantic routes and the Comet on Africa and the East. BEA bought the Comet 4B for its short-haul routes. Both airlines produced posters showing details of the aircraft, its equipment, not least their on-board comforts, and, of course, maps of their routes flown.

B·O·A·C OFFERS YOU COMET OR 707 ROLLS-ROYCE JET POWER ALL THE WAY!

ROLLS-ROYCE COMET OR 707

SERVING BRITAIN, AUSTRALIA AND THE FAR EAST

ONLY B·O·A·C OFFERS THIS CHOICE OF JETS!

SUPERLATIVE SERVICE...
from the moment you step aboard

Royal Flights also had detailed flight map guides, this one from Her Majesty the Queen's state visit to Portugal on 16 February 1957 (the photograph is of the queen leaving the aircraft on arrival at Lisbon). The map shown is of the return routing with the aircraft's flight path clearly marked and is exactly the same map as used on normal BEA flights to Portugal, although Her Majesty's copy was in a much nicer folder.

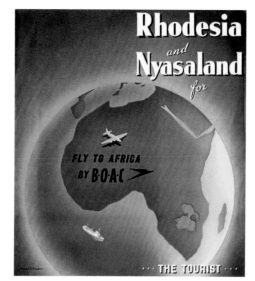

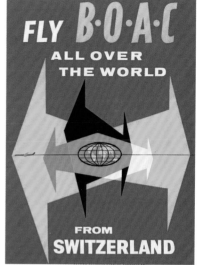

The 1950s and early 1960s was the final fling in traditional painted travel posters, although not quite on a par with the artistry of the 1930s. Maps popped up here and there, invariably an add-on rather than a main element but very relevant in getting the advertising message across. Overseas holidays were rapidly growing in popularity and not just to Mediterranean sunspots but much farther afield, places such as Africa and the Far East. The business travel opportunities that the many large overseas trade fairs offered were also not lost on BOAC. They even promoted the trade fairs around their worldwide routes, this one being for the 1954 twenty-eighth International Industries Fair in Brussels. (Top left: Beverley Pick; bottom middle: Aldo Cosomati; bottom right: Hugh Casson)

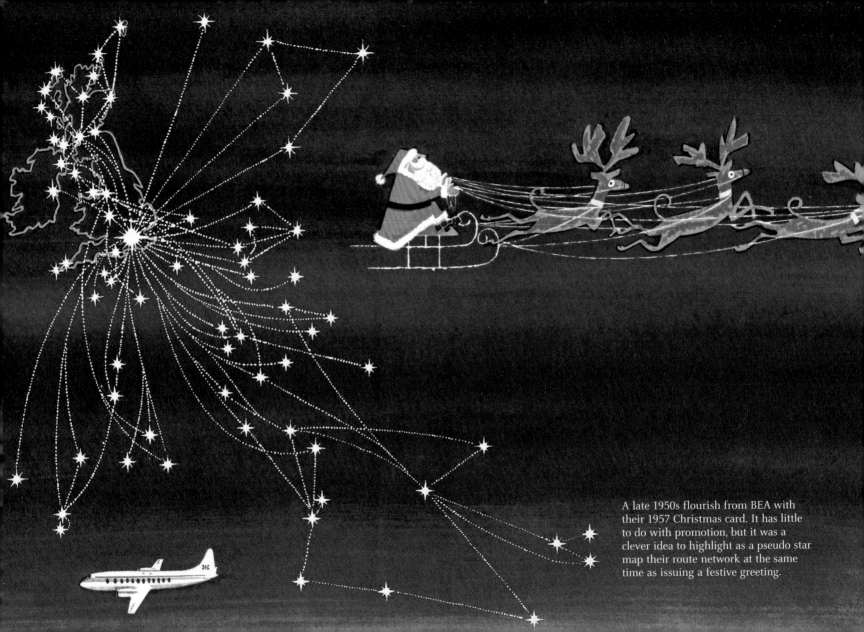

A late 1950s flourish from BEA with their 1957 Christmas card. It has little to do with promotion, but it was a clever idea to highlight as a pseudo star map their route network at the same time as issuing a festive greeting.

The later 1960s and early 1970s saw a rapid falling away of traditional painted posters and advertising and the rise of graphic and photographic art. It was a new era and not necessarily the better for that, not least as the use of maps fell away too. The inclusion of a map in a large photographic destination poster sat uneasily and was not often seen. It was the photographic image and the destination's name that was supposed to inspire, whether with an advertising message or not. The BOAC advertising strapline, 'The big round world of BOAC', and the photographic image in a large circle was the best one got at something like a globe. Even the on-board map guides and flight information became less attractive, often on lightweight paper with sometimes quite uninspiring designs, certainly not to the standards of Laszlo Moholy-Nagy in the 1930s, but then he was an exception. The world was becoming a much smaller place as many more people took to the skies for their holidays, often in far-flung places; the fact that people may not quite have known where some of these places were mattered not at all. As long as the sun was shining, that was fine. It certainly was in Lebanon in the 1960s, and Beirut was a favourite weekend destination, the Paris of the Levant.

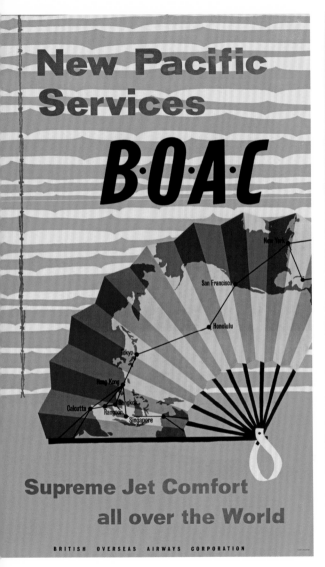

This page and opposite left: BOAC's opening up of their round-the-world services via the Pacific and the Polar route not only expanded their network but reduced journey times, as flying over the North Pole along the appropriate line of longitude was much shorter than flying around the world along a line of latitude to the same place. London to Tokyo was a good example, but even London to Los Angeles worked.

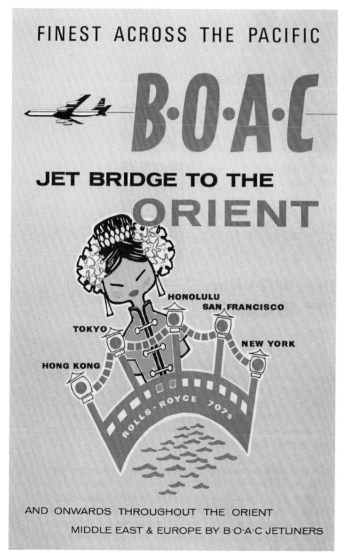

FINEST ACROSS THE PACIFIC

B·O·A·C

JET BRIDGE TO THE ORIENT

HONOLULU
SAN FRANCISCO
TOKYO
NEW YORK
HONG KONG
ROLLS-ROYCE 707s

AND ONWARDS THROUGHOUT THE ORIENT
MIDDLE EAST & EUROPE BY B·O·A·C JETLINERS

LA TRANS-SIBERIENNE
BOAC
ROUTE EXPRESS VERS L'ORIENT

LONDRES MOSCOU TOKYO

Deux fois par semaine
à partir de juin 1970
BOAC empruntera
la route la plus directe
vers le Japon

LONDRES   MOSCOU   TOKYO

Above: In the late 1960s the Russians allowed BOAC to fly to Tokyo via the Siberian routing, another shortcut, but provided a landing was made at Moscow. This rather pop art brochure from 1969 provides a neat iconic map style to the stylised outlines of the Big Ben clock tower in London, Saint Basil's Cathedral in Moscow and one of Tokyo's religious temples.

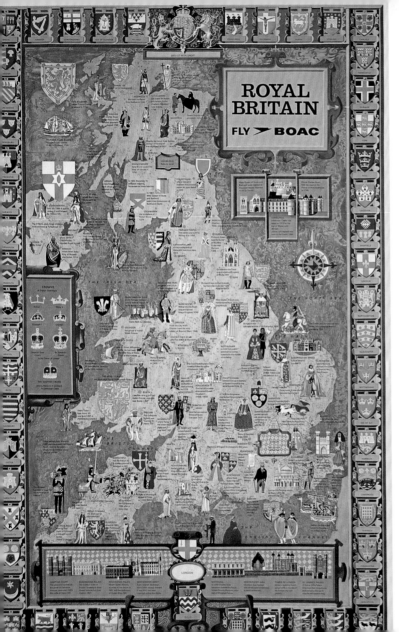

Fly to BRITAIN by
BOAC

BOURNEMOUTH, HAMPSHIRE
One of England's leading resorts. Here you can stay in fine hotels, swim from six miles of glorious golden sands, stroll in 2,000 acres of the most beautiful parks and public gardens. Bournemouth is a fashionable shopping centre, a first class touring centre (see map above), and fun to be in at any time of year.

This page: It would be churlish to suggest that BOAC did not make a fair attempt here to return to the stylised map posters of Imperial Airways with this rather attractive late 1960s map of the UK promoting travel to 'Royal Britain'. Probably produced for the American market, BOAC's most important revenue earner, it is a geographical history lesson in itself in minute detail. Enticing overseas visitors with a map of Bournemouth as a holiday destination, however, may have been more in hope than expectation, despite Bournemouth's many charms.

Opposite and overleaf: BEA and their subsidiary company British Air Services (the holding company for Northeast Airlines and Cambrian Airways) did continue to produce some interesting route and information maps, often brightly coloured, graphic representations and, in BAS's case, bearing little or no relation to reality and more along the line of a Frank Beck diagrammatic map. In fact, it was produced as part of BAS's 1970/71 annual report and accounts and is rather eye-catching, certainly of its time from an artistic perspective. BEA used a similar graphic in a 1972 poster.

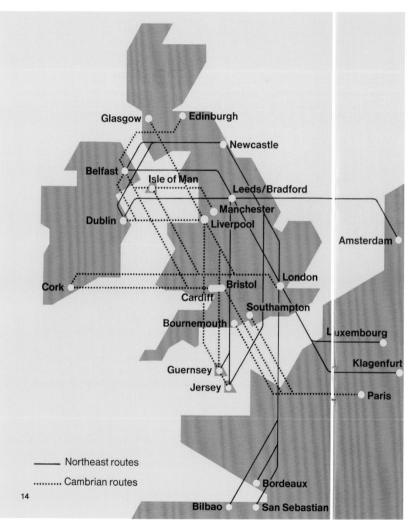

Glasgow
Edinburgh
Newcastle
Belfast
Isle of Man
Leeds/Bradford
Dublin
Manchester
Liverpool
Amsterdam
Cork
Bristol
London
Cardiff
Southampton
Bournemouth
Luxembourg
Klagenfurt
Guernsey
Jersey
Paris
Bordeaux
Bilbao
San Sebastian

——— Northeast routes
·········· Cambrian routes

14

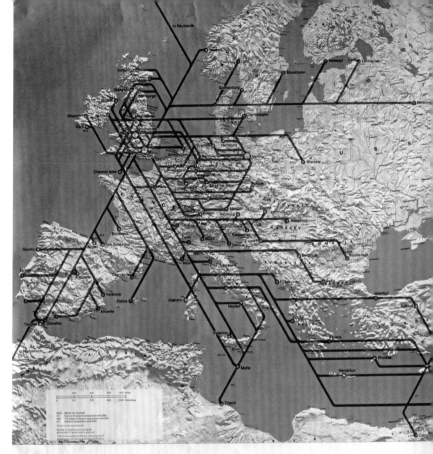

BEA
International routes 1971/2

Opposite left: Considering BEA only had European routes to map whereas BOAC had the six continents, they were certainly ahead in the later 1960s, using all manner of means to produce an interesting graphic; this one is for BEA's holiday incentives brochure. The dramatic head-on photographic shot of one of BEA's Trident aircraft over a cloudy European mainland makes an interesting background over which to outline the European and North African coastlines and the cities BEA served.

Opposite right: Several decades before the fall of the Iron Curtain, BEA operated to Moscow and a number of eastern European cities, with Zagreb coming on-line with a twice-weekly service from 1 April 1971. Although Zagreb had tourist and business potential, BEA's main reason for the operation was to benefit from the Zagreb International Trade Fair (then the third largest in the world) that operated throughout 1971. BEA's fare and information leaflet, used to promote the new service, showed on its front cover a very striking contemporary image. The graphic also had the effect of implying that BEA itself was a leader in its business and at the forefront of new ideas and technology.

BEA destinations

Shetland, Orkney, Stornoway, Wick, Inverness, Aberdeen, Edinburgh, Glasgow, Belfast, Dublin, Manchester, Shannon, Birmingham, London, Channel Isles

Bergen, Oslo, Stavanger, Gothenburg, Stockholm, Helsinki, Copenhagen, Moscow

Bremen, Hamburg, Amsterdam, Hanover, Dusseldorf, Berlin, Brussels, Cologne/Bonn, Prague, Warsaw, Frankfurt-on-Main, Munich, Stuttgart, Salzburg, Vienna, Budapest, Paris, Basle, Zurich, Geneva, Venice, Turin, Milan, Nice, Istanbul, Ankara, Dubrovnik, Rome

Oporto, Madrid, Barcelona, Gerona, Alghero, Lisbon, Valencia, Palma, Mahon, Naples, Corfu, Athens, Cyprus, Beirut, Faro, Alicante, Palermo, Catania, Tel Aviv, Tangier, Malaga, Gibraltar, Malta, Tripoli

New direct service
London–Zagreb

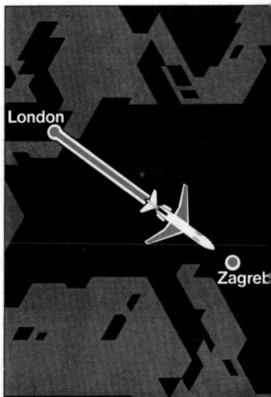

London

Zagreb

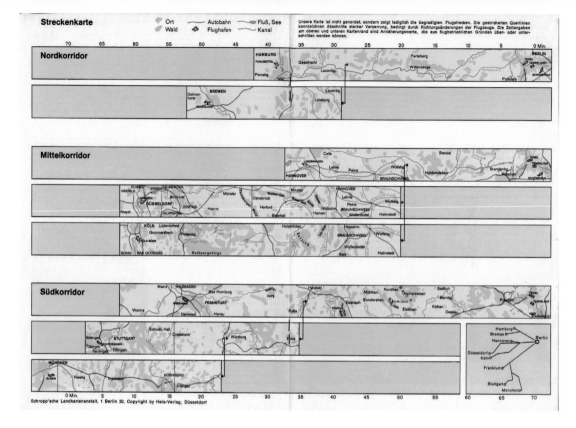

Above: BEA also operated to Berlin during the 1960s and early 1970s, a city firmly behind the Iron Curtain in what was then East Germany. Very strict flight rules were applied by the East German and Soviet authorities on flying into and out of Berlin's three airports, with only three routes allowed, known as the North, Middle and South Corridors respectively. BEA's flight and information brochure included the three corridors in a style strongly reminiscent of the strip maps of previous centuries. It was not allowed to show maps of the parts of East Germany adjacent to the corridors, so strip maps served their purpose very well.

Opposite: BOAC did continue, here and there, the use of maps as promotional mediums where they had a direct impact and not just as decoration. This late 1960s timetable map is quite different from the geography book versions that had been used for some years, adding a distinct style and interest to a solid, standard Mercator's projection of the world overlaid on what might be considered turbulent oceans. What is also striking is the spread of BOAC's route network. It certainly spanned all six continents and to an extent more significant than earlier years, albeit the Polar and Siberian routes had yet to be authorised and there was still a distinct lack of depth in routes to South America. It also predates the loss of the lucrative West African and Saudi Arabian routes licences that were subsequently taken by the UK government and given to help the UK's up-and-coming 'second force' airline, British Caledonian Airways.

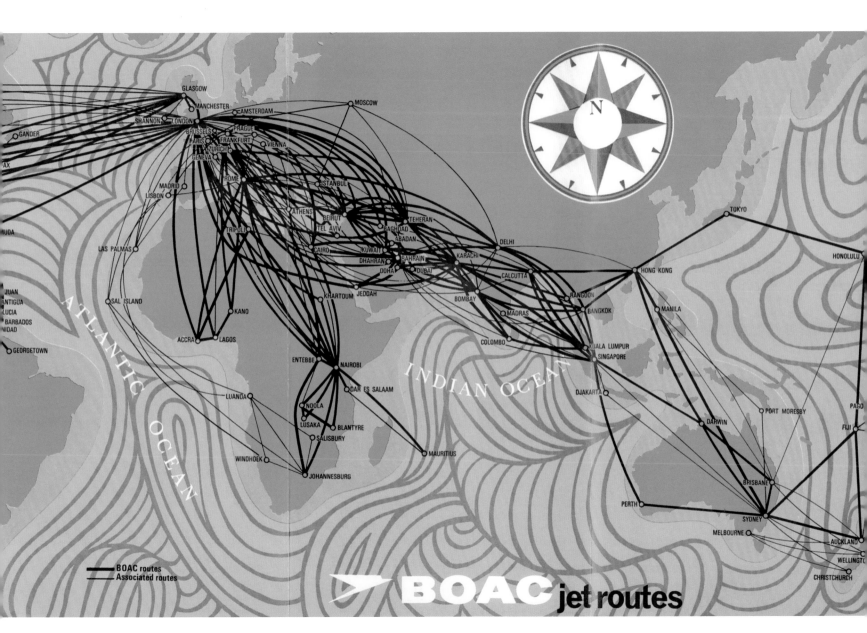

BOAC *jet routes*

FARE/TIMETABLE
WINTER 1969

Channel Airways

INTRODUCING

The Scottish Flyer

**BRITAIN'S FIRST CITY-TO-CITY
THROUGH AIR SERVICE**

Channel Airways

schedule effective 20th January
until further notice

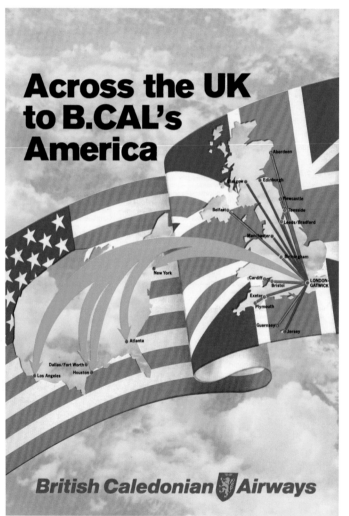

Across the UK to B.CAL's America

British Caledonian Airways

Left: British Caledonian was snapping at the heels of BOAC and British Airways throughout the 1970s and the early 1980s. Competition between airlines intensified and the UK Civil Aviation Authority leant favourably towards BCAL, granting them licences on routes once the domain of BOAC and, subsequently, British Airways. The US market was a good example, with BCAL opening services to several internal US cities, particularly in the south and south-west of the USA. This 1970s brochure cover is an eye-catching and unusual design for the time, harking back to the earlier poster period and drawn artworks of the 1950s.

Far left: BOAC and BEA during the later 1960s and early 1970s were facing competition from an increasing number of UK independent airlines. Channel Airways was a small but accomplished airline operating a wide variety of primarily short-haul UK and European scheduled services and long-haul charters. This timetable cover for the 1969/70 winter season highlights the UK's first bus-stop service, from Southend to Aberdeen with six stops on the way. The service ran during 1969 but ceased in November that year. The journey must have been remarkably tedious for any Aberdeen and Edinburgh passengers, whom I suspect would rather have opted for a direct service or the train. It also seemed very strange at the time for those of us who worked at Heathrow and Gatwick airports, traditionally the main London airports, when Southend airport started to be promoted as a 'London' airport. This was hotly disputed by the airlines operating from Heathrow and Gatwick, but the case had been made and no one thinks anything of it today; it is certainly no further away than Stansted.

BEA will be pleased to take care of your return travel
arrangements. Please ask your Hotel Concierge or the
nearest Travel Agent to contact us, unless you prefer to
drop in at one of the BEA offices listed below.

To overseas travellers planning a sojourn in Britain BEA
offer their extensive service facilities in the U.K. Please
enquire.

**Your Captain wishes you
a pleasant flight**

Basle, Centralbahnplatz 3–4, Phone 061 22 40 11
Geneva, 13, rue Chantepoulet, Phone 022 31 40 50
Zurich, Steinmühleplatz 1, Phone 01 25 54 54

Sept. 1972

Switzerland

Schweiz   Suisse   Suiza   Svizzera

No. 1 in Europe

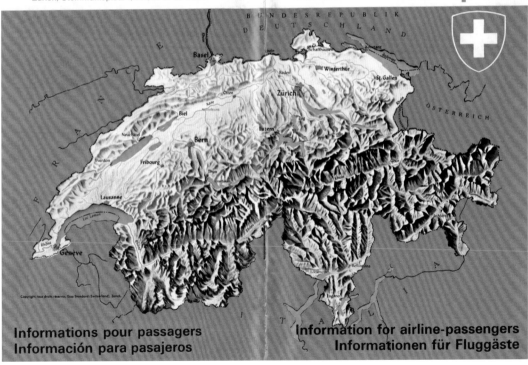

Informations pour passagers
Información para pasajeros

Information for airline-passengers
Informationen für Fluggäste

As well as producing their own information brochures
on city or country destinations, BEA and BOAC also
used local tourist brochures and overprinted them
with their logos. This one from Switzerland uses on
its cover an attractive three-dimensional map of the
country, an important destination for BEA for both
business and holiday passengers, particularly those
going skiing.

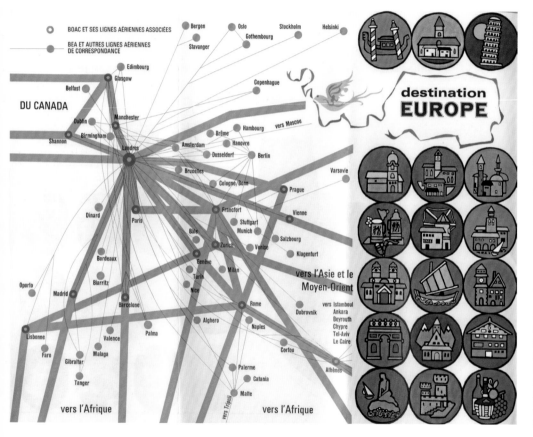

SPECTACLE INCOMPARABLE

This French-language brochure of BOAC's was for the Canadian market, promoting Europe as a destination. Its diagrammatic map is very striking suggesting BOAC's routes and those of its associated companies were the primary focus given the bold, blue route lines shown. In fact, BEA flew to far more European destinations but is given secondary focus with a mere thin spider's web of pink route lines, but this was BOAC's brochure. The graphics are quite contemporary and the main brochure montage certainly a 'spectacle incomparable'.

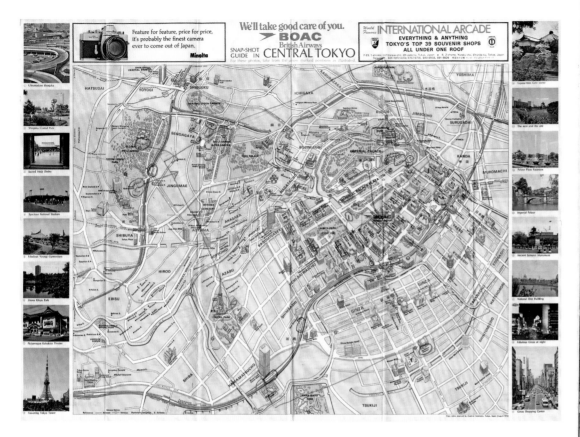

Tokyo was an important business and holiday destination for BOAC and this Tokyo street map harks back to those stylised maps of previous decades. The map cover is very much a pop art montage, an attractive, fun style often used in the 1970s that lent itself well to maps too. The cover also names both BOAC and British Airways. BOAC and BEA were to be merged to form British Airways on 31 March 1974 and, in order to encourage the transfer of brand loyalty, from 1972 the names were shown together across all advertising and promotional media.

"illustrated"
MAP OF CENTRAL
TOKYO
with colorful snap-shot guide

We'll take good care of you.
BOAC
British Airways

One booking worldwide.

Book with ease

Hotel bookings, with normal commission, can be made through any BEA or BOAC office. It's one call, one booking when you make flight and hotel arrangements at the same time.

It saves your valuable time and your clients get the assurance and backing of BEA and BOAC in every British Airways Associate Hotel.

Book with confidence

Travellers, who sometimes feel that an unknown hotel represents a risk, can rely on the recommendation of two British airlines in which they already have confidence. If a British Standard for international hotels was ever wanted, BEA and BOAC have defined it.

Value—the prime standard

BAAH hotels are by no means stereotyped. They offer variety in every respect except the most important one —value for money, and that is standard. British Airways Associate Hotels range from over a thousand bedrooms to the club-like atmosphere of a 50-bedroom lodge. Locations vary from the centres of world capitals to a hotel with a Fijian Island all to itself.

From business conferences to deep-sea fishing, you'll find everything to satisfy your clients' requirements.

And to ensure consistency of character in this diverse field, BAAH selects the management partners best suited to run each type of hotel.

If you would like further information, please contact your nearest BEA or BOAC office.

British Airways Associate Hotels

Left: Just on the cusp of the BOAC/BEA merger, British Airways Associated Hotels issued this lavishly illustrated pop art brochure promoting its overseas hotels. Most were on the BOAC network and, in fact, BAAH were a subsidiary company of BOAC and, subsequently, British Airways. The pop art Boeing 747 was also the lead image for BOAC's Poundstretcher travel promotion.

Opposite and overleaf spread: British Airways' first route maps were issued in 1974. They were rather flimsy fold-up versions with a nice enough globe and contemporary graphics on the front cover, but another of those real geography books of a world map inside. Using a Gall's stereographic projection to lay out its worldwide routes over several pages in a traditional three-dimensional and quite usable format, a separate and complex diagrammatic map was also included. Quite why a Gall's projection was used is not clear. Although it does provide a more balanced view of the world by minimising distortion, I'm not sure that this makes much difference to what is being shown other than to show more of the world on less paper. The diagrammatic map, however, does clearly emphasise the size and extent of British Airways' route network. By combining the networks of BOAC and BEA, and even allowing for the removal of duplicated routes, British Airways could claim it now had the most routes of any other airline worldwide. Given the airline had nearly 200 destinations, the claim may well have been true and it is interesting to compare the growth of the company's route network since the very early days of its predecessor Imperial Airways. In less than fifty years, British Airways had grown from around five European routes and one in the Middle East to over 200.

ROUTE MAP

British airways

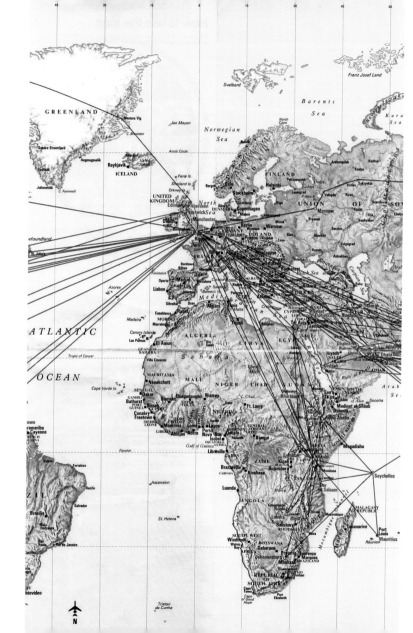

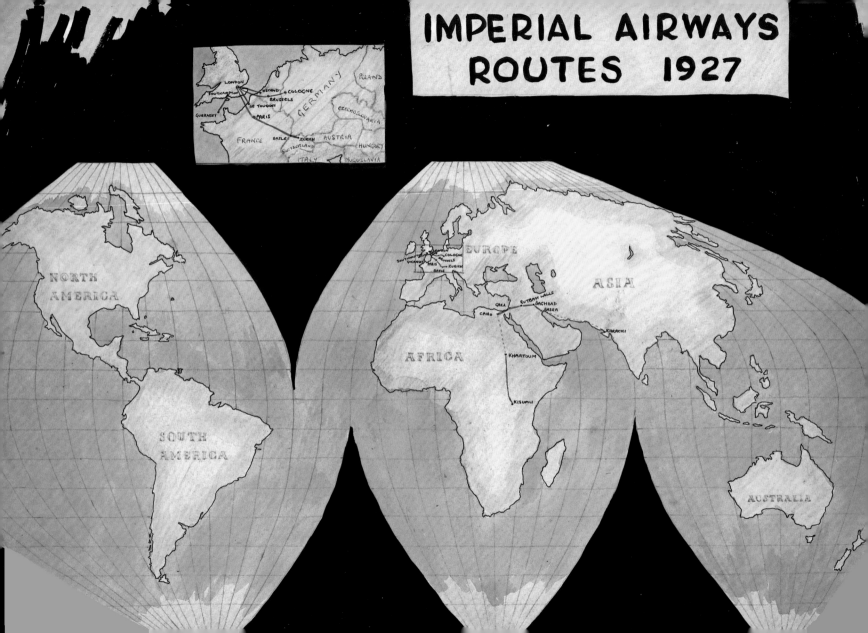

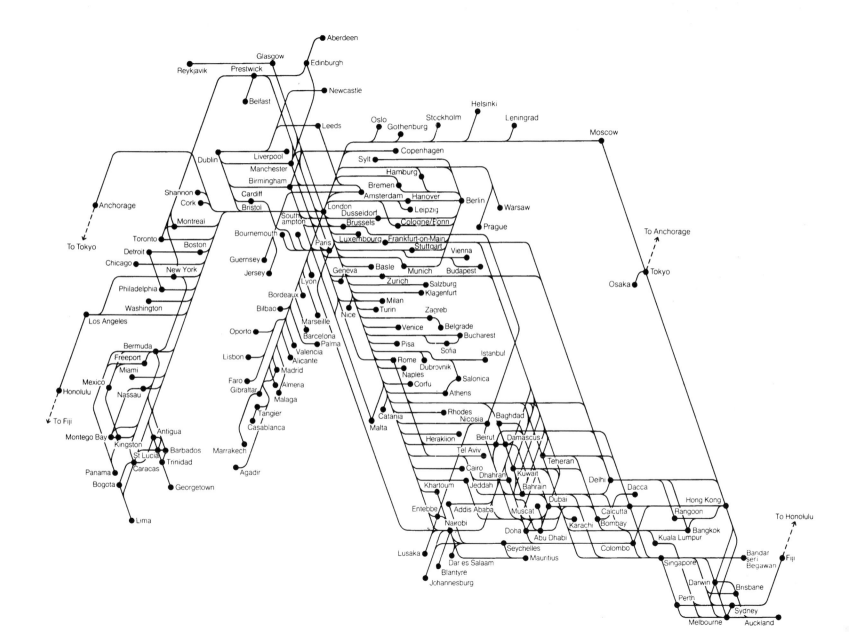

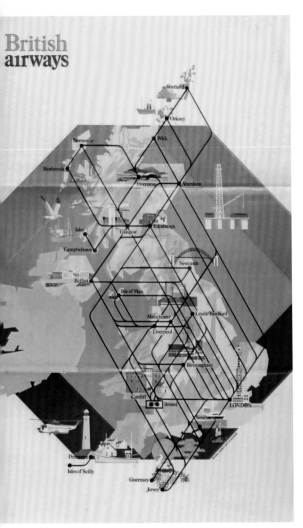

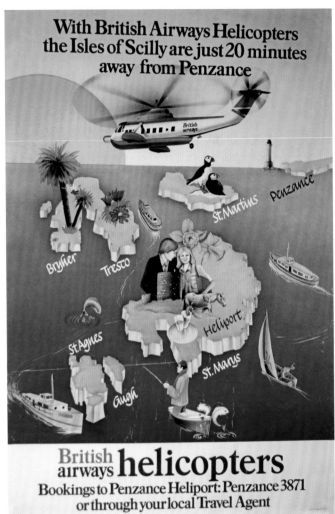

Far left: One of British Airways' first advertising posters in 1975 under its 'Fly the Flag' promotion used a diagrammatic route network overlaid on an outline of the UK with almost pop art images representing sights of the cities or industries located across the UK. The blue-and-red lozenge shape in the background was the identifying graphic for the 'Fly the Flag' campaign but, apart from being an eye-catching graphic, I'm not sure that the message was at all clear other than that it was from the new airline.

Left: British Airways Helicopters was a subsidiary company of British Airways operating a variety of services, from North Sea oilfield charters to a quite successful scheduled helicopter service between Penzance in Cornwall and the Isles of Scilly. This quite attractive graphic from the mid-1970s might well encourage holidaymakers to use the service rather than the much slower ferry, and many did. Helicopters were a legacy from BEA, who had operated all manner of helicopter services from the late 1940s up to the merger with BOAC in 1974. As British Airways began to economise its business in the early 1980s it became clear that helicopters were a distraction from its main scheduled service operation and the subsidiary was sold.

It is quite difficult to find maps from the late 1970/early 1980 period. The medium appears to have fallen out of favour but quite why is unclear. Advertising media was all about photography and graphics of one form or another, and maybe the world was just becoming a better known place so there was no need to use maps or globes to highlight an airline's route network. Maybe British Airways was still finding its way and its promotional direction was becoming stale and needed redirecting. The airline certainly needed redirecting, and that process began with the appointment of Sir John King (later Lord King of Wartnaby) as chairman in February 1981 and a massive shake-up over the following three years. Saatchi & Saatchi were appointed in 1983 as British Airways' new advertising agency and made an immediate impact with a new campaign based on the theme of 'The world's favourite airline'. Not just a map but the world, seen (digitally, anyway) from outer space, became a central part of the campaign. (Saatchi & Saatchi)

It's the way we *make you feel* that makes us the world's favourite.

BRITISH AIRWAYS

The above diagram shows British Airways departure points from the UK to the USA and Canada in the centre. The middle ring shows directly served destinations and the outer ring shows all USAir connections with code share routes highlighted in bold.

BRITISH AIRWAYS

Far left: The use of a globe, this time with a smiling face, continued the 'world's favourite' theme for several years. This poster is from the mid-1980s, but rather than marking the resurrection of the use of maps and globes it was merely being used as a medium to make an advertising point and nothing else. As the self-appointed 'world's favourite airline', it was almost as if it implied British Airways flew everywhere and everyone. As research had shown that British Airways flew more people to more places than any other airline (hence the strapline 'The world's favourite airline'), the implication is not too far off the truth. Maybe there was no need then to know exactly where places were or people came from. On-board aircraft technology was now providing personal overhead screens and the early versions of the en-route moving map and its jerky aircraft image had replaced the passenger map books of old. The moving map was virtually useless as an accurate vision of where one was, but merely a mild comforter that one's journey actually was progressing to its destination.

Above right: Is it a map, a globe or a rather confusing circle of city place names? Titled as a diagram showing British Airways' departure points from the UK (easy to see they are Glasgow, Manchester, Heathrow or Gatwick) to cities in the USA and Canada, listed in the inner ring (fairly easy to see), it then shows in its outer ring all of US Air's connections (difficult to see without glasses and a lot of neck-twisting). US Air was in the early 1980s a partner airline of British Airways serving many US destinations. While this diagram does in a way use a combination of a simple map of the UK with a graphic that allows a lot of information to be shown, it has nothing to do with geography or art but just a designer's imagination and little else. In the digital age, many images seem to be just that. Unless continental drift has sped up since I last looked, I suggest the designer's imagination in placing the UK at the North Pole is rather over the top.

TWENTY-FIRST-CENTURY AIR TRAVEL

When I first started work at BOAC on 6 June 1966, large maps of the world adorned many of the company's office walls. We even had a rather splendid antique globe – well it looked antique to me, in the anteroom to the boardroom. That globe still graces what is now called The Hub at British Airways' shiny corporate headquarters at Harmondsworth near Heathrow airport, but I doubt it is used much now, if at all. Maps rarely grace any office walls either, and their sad demise following the turn of the millennium is rather the opposite of what was once an overt and wide use of maps in the company. When I joined BOAC, before Google and the internet, geographical knowledge was considered important in the airline business. We were expected to know where at least major countries and places actually were and for those less certain maps provided that instant and reassuring confirmation.

It all seems such a long time ago now. Today, in-flight magazines occasionally might show a map in an article, say, about a new destination, but the days are gone of detailed and colourful descriptive paper maps made available to passengers to show them the way. There is also the occasional advertisement showing a map or globe of sorts, just so we don't forget that air travel is largely an international business spanning the globe, but quite where on the globe does not seem to matter in getting the message across, subliminally or otherwise.

There are consolations, however. The twenty-first-century version of the seat-back screen's 'moving map' is actually a pretty good representation of a mini-aircraft moving smoothly across a pretty good map of the world – much more watchable and accurate than the jerky earlier version that was almost mesmerising in itself as one watched it and tried to will it to move faster to journey's end. The new GPS-driven device is also now augmented, on some aircraft, by software that allows a passenger to browse a digital map of the world and interrogate its physical features, almost like Google Earth. Once on-board real-time connectivity is implemented, and it surely will be, I suspect that the pleasure of a real map will be replaced by a digital screen, as it has done for much of twenty-first century life. I suspect that someone, somewhere, will be developing an on-board app for it.

Operationally, the dearth of maps continues. The days of large-scale navigation charts and wooden boxes of maps in the cockpit are long gone. In this domain that's to be welcomed. The old ways of hasty celestial sightings taken in an aircraft bouncing along in unstable air is not to be recommended. Modern technology, particularly the relatively recent availability of highly accurate navigation by GPS, is the only way forward.

In another one hundred years I doubt this book could be repeated, if at all, with anything like the number of images of the use of maps in aviation. Maps will still exist for specialist aviation functions I'm sure,

but the days of folded maps in seat pockets showing the route to be followed are now long gone, and digitised versions rule the skies. I really liked those old route maps. It was always so much fun looking from an aircraft window at over 30,000 feet on a clear day map-reading one's way across the world map in hand. I now have to rely on memory, not a good idea, or invest in a tablet; I don't think my *Times Atlas* will fit on board. That said, the new moving map goes a long way towards compensating for the pleasures of the real thing. With digital pointers allowing one to zoom in and out with different levels of detail, it might yet satisfy even passengers such as myself. I remain, as ever, optimistic.

Bartle Bogle Hegarty.

This spread: A good thing about including twenty-first-century advertising is one can ask the designer why they used a globe. The ads themselves are all clever graphics and Photoshop make-believe, but that does not detract from their story-telling effect and eye-catching design, or at least the prompting of thoughts of travel and exploration – and why not on British Airways. A globe is thought provoking in itself and an appropriate representation for an airline such as British Airways with a truly global reach and international level of customer service. And what about the message – 'The world is on sale'? It is a literal call that British Airways can get you to anywhere in the world at a discounted price, at least for the period of the sale. Advertising messages are of their time but the globe is a universal symbol and crosses the centuries. The use of a globe is indeed thought provoking and does imply a global reach or, in the case of Imperial Airways and its use of the Union Flag nearly one hundred years ago, a dominion over empire. In that sense not a lot appears to have changed, except for a changed world order and the design opportunities digitisation has provided. (Left: Leandro Farina/Bartle Bogle Hegarty)

CONSTANT CLIMATE
PRECISION TIME AND TEMPERATURE CONTROL FOR
PHARMACEUTICAL AND LIFE SCIENCE SHIPMENTS

IAG

IAG Cargo

Left: I think this is a clever bit of advertising on a par with some of the best of the past. It's from IAG Cargo, a company part of the International Airlines Group that now owns, among others, British Airways. Using modern climate maps and the message of offering a constant temperature for scientific shipments, the aircraft silhouette slicing a cold blue gash through the yellow heat of the Sahara Desert makes an immediate impact, as all good adverts should. Maybe the delights of the modernists and their successors has not really passed us by and in one hundred years another book, but of twenty-first-century creativity in map ads, will be possible. (IAG Cargo/Bartle Bogle Hegarty)

Next four pages: Just to make the point about the huge advances in the development of the digital seat-back map and its abilities, I had to include these four images. One looks suspiciously like the old, clunky system of yesteryear, with a small aeroplane moving across the face of the globe. Don't be fooled. The clue lies in some little pointer buttons just off screen. Press these and the map is transformed into a journey of virtual reality as one crosses mountain ranges and oceans, across London (almost as clear as on a fine day – who needs a window seat with this system) and finally landing at Heathrow on runway 9. Right. I think I'm being converted. (GeoFusion/Worldsat/Thales Avionics/Kosmos)

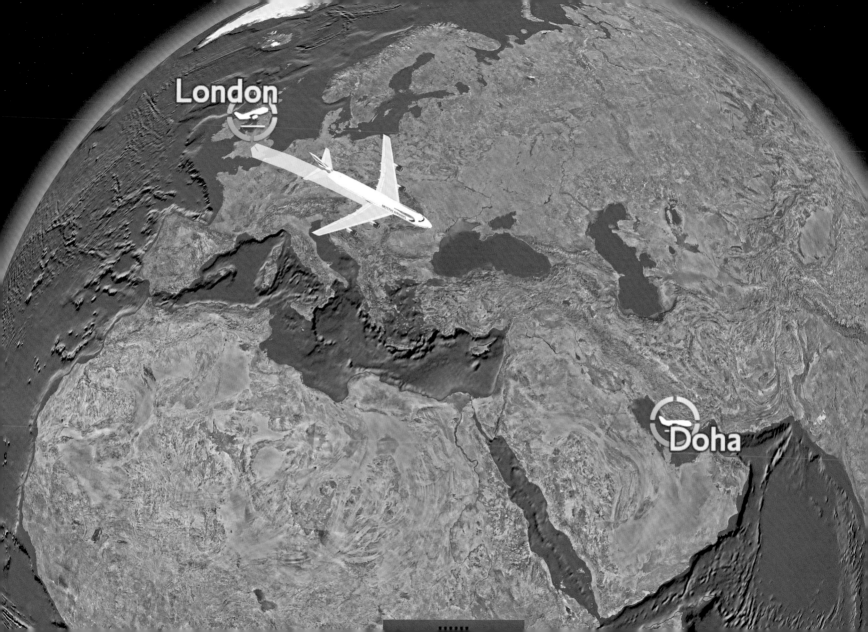

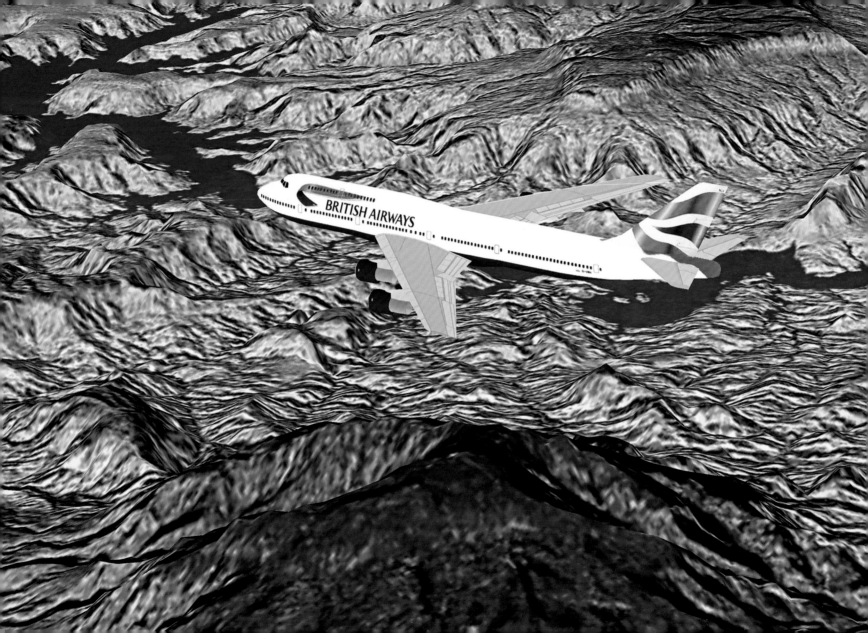

London